MOMENTS OF TRANSITION

Processes of Structuring in Man, Society and Art

J. Russell Reaver

UNIVERSITY
PRESS OF
AMERICA

Copyright © 1982 by
University Press of America,Inc.
P.O. Box 19101, Washington, D.C. 20036

All rights reserved

Printed in the United States of America

ISBN (Perfect): 0-8191-2546-6
ISBN   (Cloth): 0-8191-2545-8

Library of Congress Number: 82-40086

ACKNOWLEDGMENTS

Chapter I is a much expanded development of an address given in August, 1979, at the Seventh Congress of the International Society for Folk-Narrative Research in Edinburgh, Scotland, and published as an article "Socio-Psychic Levels of Oral Narration," Fabula: Journal of Folktale Studies, 22 (1981), 64-73.

Chapter VI first appeared as "Musical Structure in the Fiction of Bellow, Malamud, and Updike," Interdisciplina, 1 (1976), 42-55. It is reproduced here by permission of Dr. John F. Spratt, editor of the SLM Press.

"Attitudes are nothing, madam, --- 'tis the transition
from one attitude to another --- like the preparation
and resolution of the discord into harmony, which is
all in all." Laurence Sterne, Tristram Shandy, 4:6,
276-277

"Beauty is the moment of transition, as if the form
were just ready to flow into other forms. . . . It is
necessary in music, when you strike a discord, to let
down the ear by an intermediate note or two to the
accord again." Ralph Waldo Emerson, The Conduct of
Life, 292-293

"The universe exists only in transit, or we behold it
shooting the gulf from past to future. . .; not in his
goals but in his transitions man is great." Ralph
Waldo Emerson, "Powers and Laws of Thought," Natural
History of Intellect, 59-60

"Because of its notion of dynamic patterns, generated
by change and transformation, the I Ching is perhaps
the closest analogy to S-matrix theory in Eastern
thought. In both systems, the emphasis is on processes
rather than objects. In S-matrix theory, these processes are the particle reactions that give rise to all
the phenomena in the world of hadrons. In the I Ching,
the basic processes are called 'the changes' and are
seen as essential for an understanding of all natural
phenomena. . . . The important point, however, is not
this accidental similarity, but the fact that both
modern physics and ancient Chinese thought consider
change and transformation as the primary aspect of
nature, and see the structures and symmetries generated
by the changes as secondary." Fritjof Capra, The Tao
of Physics, 281-283

Music "is no symbol of time or process, mental or physical, Newtonian or Bergsonian; it is process. And
perhaps we can say it is the closest thing to pure process, to happening as such, to change abstracted from
anything that changes." Monroe Beardsley, Aesthetics,
338

TABLE OF CONTENTS

INTRODUCTION

I

In this study I show at the outset the socio-
psychic levels of oral narration. These levels,
described as the Rhema, Epos, Mythos, and Logos, com-
bine a sense of social meaning and personal order. In
varied degrees such narratives as the tall tale, the
ghost story, the historical anecdote, the epic, and
the myth demonstrate associations of the external world
in nature and society with the internal world in psychic experiences fundamental to all literary art.
Moving by dynamic transitions from one form of expression to another, these narratives illustrate the breadth
and depth in the artistic processes of structuring man
and society.

Such imaginative structures appear only remotely
to the monster Grendel in John Gardner's contemporary
novel of this animal groping toward becoming human.
Within the traditional involutions and evolutions of
the zodiac, Grendel is stirred in spite of his subhuman
nature to grasp some significance in the courtly Epos
and Mythos underlying the superficial Rhema level of
his existence. Before the moment of death, Grendel has
a vision of the ultimate shape of life as the human
Logos that has impelled his attention through the singing of the Shaper's songs.

In the Winnebago Indian heroic cycle of tales, the
Trickster emerges farther than Grendel from his animal
nature but for a long while continues to fool himself
and others by his shape-shifting to gain pleasure for
himself or control over his natural and human environment. Through a shock to his pride, he begins to emerge
from his infantile level toward a maturity that at last
transforms the cleverness in the Trickster into the will
to aid his people.

This kind of savior role appears most effectively
in modern fantasy through the devotion of Gandalf in
J. R. R. Tolkien's trilogy to rescue the "Third Age"
from evil powers. In his evolution, Gandalf experiences
transitions to higher moral values beyond those of the
Trickster. Gandalf's wizardry evolves into the compassion of a Bodhisattva returned from death to save his
companions from the agony of life.

The narratives of Grendel, the Trickster, and Gandalf center on patterns of departure, initiation, and return. Such transitions appear both in their social roles and in their psychic developments. The farther out such figures go in their search for meaning, the deeper they go in their discovery of themselves.

The sense of polar opposites, within a whole society or a particular individual, creates much of the tensions felt in epic or mythic narratives. In contemporary Greece, Nikos Kazantzakis dramatizes the stresses between the Apollonian and the Dionysian phases of experience in Zorba and the Boss. These tensions are resolved through religious relations between Apollo and Dionysus with their associations in myth and music, represented in the forms of the dithyramb and the paean. On all levels of experience, music offers a model of structure in its most abstract qualities. The reliance on Buddhist-Tantric tradition resolves opposites for the Boss, who goes beyond Zorba in his awareness of his own humanity, an interplay between the irrational and the rational, the Dionysian dithyramb and the Apollonian paean.

Musical kinds of resolutions appear in novels like Saul Bellow's The Adventures of Augie March (theme and variations), Bernard Malamud's The Assistant (arch-sonata), and John Updike's The Centaur (madrigal).

The social transitions Thorkild Jacobsen found within ancient Mesopotamia (The Treasures of Darkness) and the evolutions of human intelligence Carl Sagan described (The Dragons of Eden) suggest a correspondence between man's outer and inner worlds, united through the ability of imagination to achieve structures of meaning from perceived reality.

The effects of the Rhema, Epos, Mythos, and Logos levels, repeatedly appearing from folk narrative traditions through sophisticated fictional techniques, have been finely structured as implicit musical experiences. These narratives gain some of their emotional and esthetic strength through their analogies to such Western musical forms as the madrigal and the arch-sonata, whether or not the artists' creative imaginations were always conscious of the musical associations. Searching for order, the imagination finds ways of structuring that create narratives in methods conventionally associated with musical art, but not restricted to it.

Eastern musical style appears in Yukio Mishima's vision of the cosmos as a Japanese koto, a form suggested in the dream analogy of Kiyoaki, who plays the role of an improvising voice above the drum beat of rationalistic Honda and the elegant recitative of Satoko. Mishima's narrative gives a wider vista of musical experience beyond Western forms. In his Oriental view of modern man's sterility, Mishima brings this study full circle.

The forms that literature takes reflect the functions of human experience, the narrative levels of the Rhema, Epos, Mythos, and Logos being found and disclosed in esthetic forms intensifying them in their revelations of dynamic moments of transition in the processes of structuring man, society, and art.

II

My uses of the socio-psychic levels of narrative, together with analogies to musical structure, offer ways of responding to literary experience beyond currently popular critical theories, such as "reception aesthetics" popularized in the United States by Stanley Fish's Surprised by Sin: The Reader's Paradise Lost (1967), as well as the "Geneva Criticism" introduced to Americans through J. Hillis Miller's views found in his critical works from Charles Dickens: The World of his Novels (1959) to Thomas Hardy: Distance and Desire (1970), which attempt to give a portrait of a writer's consciousness, and the "Buffalo Criticism" associated with Norman Holland, whose study, Five Readers Reading (1975), focuses on the interactions between reader and text. But inevitably there are some overlappings between my methods and theirs. Every critic must make his own choices depending on his interests and concerns. My methods are perhaps less "subjectivist" than those of Fish, Miller, or Holland. At the same time my approach to literature continues to see values in perceiving significant structures that reveal human meanings. While we differ in the emphasis given to subjective responses and formal literary qualities, we share something in being more ahistorical than many American traditions of historical and objective formalist criticism. While I am interested in discovering common denominators within psychic levels of creation and response resulting in structures resembling muscial forms, I have tried to take historical settings or motivations into account whenever I

xi

thought they were appropriate. As a result, I draw
upon some "spiritual" aspects of the Geneva Critic or
"scientific" views of the Buffalo Critic if they apply
to my own purposes. I also share some of the "psycho-
sociological" attitude of the Receptionist Critic. But
my eclectic methods are not accidental or fortuitous
any more than my selections of texts extending from
oral tales to recent novels are casual or incidental.
On the contrary, my examples were carefully chosen to
show how some further contributions might be made to
literary understanding when levels of storytelling and
musical structuring are taken into account.

In his introduction to Directions for Criticism:
Structuralism and Its Alternatives (Madison: University
of Wisconsin Press, 1977), Murray Krieger discloses the
increasing dislike of modern "structuralist" criticism
among the critical fashions in the twentieth century,
which Hayden White labels for his symposium the "Normal," the "Reductive," the "Inflationary," the "Exis-
tentialist," the "Generalized," and the "Absurdist"
(pp. 18-19). Vincent B. Leitch neatly reviews the chief
emphases and contradictions of contemporary criticism
in "A Primer of Recent Critical Theories," College
English, 39 (October, 1977), 138-152. In "Fear and
Trembling at Yale" (The American Scholar, 46 [Autumn,
1977], 467-478), Gerald Graff describes the suffering
or anxiety of many recent critics who, feeling futility
and despair when trying to say anything valuable about
literature, end by assuming that the reader of criticism is interested in hearing a lengthy confession of
the critic's own struggles. Graff concludes: "We
should have to discard some of the central ideas of
literary modernism--for this is what malaise of criticism finally amounts to: modernism weary of itself
and knowing it, but not ready to strike out in a different direction" (p. 478). Like Robert Scholes, however, I believe that structural studies have a future
beyond the narrow formalisms that tend to be mechanical
and nearly nonhuman. To Scholes the "properly structuralist imagination" must be keyed to the future since
imagination itself is concerned with achieving significant structures that point to human capacities for
understanding the present and projecting the future.
Such a view is genuinely creative as Scholes develops
it in Structuralism in Literature (New Haven: Yale
University Press, 1974). I must finally confess to
sharing with Saul Bellow in his Nobel lecture the conviction that there are values in literature relying
on true impressions from our own human depths, the

glimpses that Proust or Tolstoy found were the essence
of their lives. "A novel," Bellow claims, "moves back
and forth between the world of objects, of actions, of
appearances, and that other world from which these 'true
impressions' come and which moves us to believe that
the good we hang on to so tenaciously--in the face of
evil, so obstinately--is no illusion." ("The Nobel
Lecture," The American Scholar, 46 [Summer, 1977], 325.)
By going beyond the "currently paralyzed debates" that
Frank Lentricchia describes in After the New Criticism
(Chicago: The University of Chicago Press, 1980, p.
351), we can discover the human being more fully as the
focus of social and psychic dynamisms that make his
life and art worthy of renewed attention.

CHAPTER I

SOCIO-PSYCHIC LEVELS OF ORAL NARRATIVE:

STRUCTURES OF THE IMAGINATION

As the socio-psychic levels in the world's stories, we may use, for this study, the Greek terms Rhema, Epos, Mythos, and Logos. In general, the meanings of these terms as I am using them depend on recognizing an interplay of social and personal responses to narratives. On the Rhema level we find what I call the more reportorial or journalistic kinds of stories, giving us statements of surface truths in the familiar world of our everyday lives in time and place. Even here, however, we may not be concerned entirely with dependable reporting but rather already with degrees of fantasy or stretching of reality as we think we know it. On the Epos level we meet the epic hero, the central figure in our epics and cyclic romances, the hero having in himself an embodiment of national or racial values. In the Mythos we discover a further concentration, both in meaning and in manner of storytelling, because the subject of the Mythos as it appears in the narratives of creation, rebirth, or polarity concentrates on the structuring of binary opposites, such as the good and evil, the light and darkness, birth and death of the world that account for the aspects of nature and society as man tends to find them in the polar extremities of his experience. Beyond such narratives, representing what I take to be a central effort of explaining reality on the Mythos level as they project human hope and fear, we can further focus in on the Logos level, containing the non-discursive symbols of experience, the remembered and highly charged images becoming the archetypal metaphors, sometimes mandalas, which subsume in themselves the moral-spiritual experiences of the human race. This psychic level indicates something of an intuitive understanding of ultimate life origins, characterizing a traditional religious view, as in the familiar text equating Logos with Word in the Greek of the Gospel According to St. John: "In the beginning was the Word, and the Word was with God, and the Word was God." In any event, we are dealing with psychic constructions of great human significance, which, from the Hindu perspective, is the monosyllable AUM of the Vedas, or the result of the triangle: ideation-wording-utterance.[1]

To suggest now an analogy between these narrative levels, which we have broadly seen, and internal psy-

1

chic levels, we may suggest the Rhema level is that of
our conscious psychic life, of our everyday world. The
Epos level is a kind of mediating phase, which moves us
somewhat away from our ordinary, conscious, deliberate
experience into a sort of preconscious level, where our
attention is displaced to some extent from daily concerns to matters of deeper traditional values inherited
from past social, racial groups. In the Mythos level
we reach an even deeper level of significance that may
be analogous to a personal unconscious, where, in the
narratives of the creation of nature and man and the
stresses between people and their environment, we have
central configurations that help us realize the ultimate significance of creation, but they become conscious
to us only as they are able to bridge the preconscious
level and emerge into our full consciousness. Although
colored by our personal experience in our special circumstances of time and place in historical culture,
they belong to the deeper, more spontaneous levels of
creativity. Finally, the Logos level suggests what
Carl Jung called the collective unconscious, which I
am using in the general sense of representing the tendency of mankind to create archetypal figures, varying
from culture to culture and time to time in specific
content but still suggesting that geography of the
imagination that centers itself in the circle as the
basic symbol of unity within variety.

To illustate this theoretical introduction, I will
use primarily American and Balinese materials that I am
most personally associated with in fieldwork and study
although many other examples of worldwide folktales will
be referred to. We may look first at some narratives on
the Rhema level, examples of tales we can find in Zora
Neale Hurston's Mules and Men, her classic collection of
folktales from the black people of Florida, where we
find a typical storytelling session among these people
who are trying to outdo each other in tales they are
telling about their life in central Florida. We find
the people one day discussing the kinds of snakes they
have been afraid of in their rural community, and one
person named Presley begs them not to tell any more
about snakes, he says, because he's so afraid of them
that he will never sleep that night if he hears any
more tales, and when he says he's "skeered" of snakes,
one Cliff Ulmer cuts him off: "Who ain't?"

"It sho is gettin' hot. Ah'll be glad when we git
to de lake so Ah kin find myself some shade."

"Man, youse two miles from dat lake yet, and otherwise it ain't hot today," said Joe Wiley. "He ain't
seen it hot, is he Will House?"

"Naw, Joe, when me and you was hoboing down in
Texas it was so hot till we saw old stumps and logs
crawlin' off in de shade."

Eugene Oliver said, "Aw dat wasn't hot. Ah seen
it so hot till two cakes of ice left the ice house and
went down the street and fainted."

Arthur Hopkins put in: "Ah knowed two men who
went to Tampa all dressed up in new blue serge suits and
it was so hot dat when de train pulled into Tampa two
blue serge suits got off de train. De men had done
melted out of 'em."

Will House said, "Dat wasn't hot. Dat was chilly
weather. Me and Joe Wiley went fishin' and it was so
hot dat before we got to de water, we met de fish coming
swimming up de road in dust."

"Dat's a fact, too," added Joe Wiley. "Ah remember dat day well. It was so hot dat Ah struck a match
to light my pipe and set the lake afire. Burnt half
of it, den took de water that was left and put out de
fire."[2]

This conversation depends on what we recognize as
"tall tales," the stories that stretch the truth until
it nearly tears, but still intending in this atmosphere
to convince the listener that these behaviors of man
and nature are to be believed. Of course as society
becomes more sophisticated the storyteller cannot
expect to fool a greenhorn in the crowd, as the tales
used to be able to accomplish in early frontier America,
where conditions were often extreme and entirely
unknown and unexpected to the newcomer, and therefore
the hoodwinking of the immigrant into the local society
could be accomplished by these stretchers to the amuse-
ment of the initiates and the eventual embarrassment
of the innocents. The main point, however, whether
you believe them or not, is that while you are listening to the tales you are expected to have a sense of
reality: these events really did happen. Now, when
you cannot accept them scientifically, you can at
least enjoy the art of exaggeration, a manner of main-
taining suspense and a self-consistency within the
premises of the tales; they have their own kind of

3

internal logic.

If we look at the structures of such narratives, we find further ways in which we experience reality in the tall-tale world. In my collection of over 2,000 manuscripts of tall tales collected from people throughout the United States and now housed in the folklore archives of the Library of Congress, one of the favorite tales is "the wonderful hunt" in which all sorts of animals and birds on the ground, in the trees, in the air, on the water are killed with one shot, but many fall in the river, where the hunter must go to rescue them and finds after he wades out that he has also caught numerous fish in his boots, still, as he is bending over to get them, a button snaps off his pants and kills another animal or bird for good measure. This structure typifies a tale rising vertically by multiplying essentially the same kind of episode: the tale teller rubs the same spot as long as his listeners can stand it throughout this vertical vertigo.[3] On the other hand, in the whole body of tall tales popular in the United States, you can find a kind of horizontal sweep of taletelling, representing a cause and effect relationship within time and place that gives this sort of internal structuring. By horizontal sweep I mean the effect involved in the typical tale of the amazing swelling of a tree when a snake bites it, then the building of a barn from the large lumber supply, with all going well until the barn is painted with turpentine and the chemical reaction with the snake venom makes the barn shrink and all the cows are killed before the farmer can get them out. The brittle comedy of this tale must be maintained so that we do not feel the sad fate of the animals. The story must be clipped short with no reflection over the result. Our attention is fixed, rather, in this horizontal sweep, on the movement within a world of diachronic events, shooting like an arrow across the landscape straightforwardly from one cause to its effect, which becomes a cause for another effect.[4] When such tales are told as a string of episodes centering on a local character, they suggest the beginnings of the picaresque narrative, as in the repertory of Jones Tracy of Mount Desert Island, Maine.[5]

Objectively, such tales, of course, cannot be thought of as exclusively realistic but already a combination of reality and fantasy, or, if you like, a movement from reality as we ordinarily understand it into a world of fantasy. This condition suggests that

4

most of the statements taken as fact about life really exist already in what we loosely call "gossip:" there is hardly any fact of national or personal interest that is told, whether a love affair, a car accident, a foreign battle, or a financial scandal, that doesn't soon get reworked in its retelling so that in a few days' time no one can recognize his own report. We tend to reevaluate and editorialize even the most trivial events as our emotions play on them and lead us to create our own interpretation. Everyone yields to the temptation to become a storyteller, without realizing how tall most of his tales are.

Another favorite kind of storytelling, particularly in the United States, in addition to the tall tale, is the ghost tale. One such story circulating in the metropolitan lore of New York City and showing this movement from the factual to the fantastic or from the realistic to the imaginative is one about a dream, already a displacement from waking reality.

The tale begins with a young woman dreaming she has come to a lovely house in the country and tries to enter it, but always at the moment when an old man with a long beard opens the door she wakes up.

> A few weeks later, the young lady was motoring to Litchfield for a week-end party, when she suddenly tugged at the driver's sleeve, and begged him to stop. There, at the right of the concrete highway, was the country lane of her dreams! "Wait for me a few moments," she pleaded, and, her heart beating wildly, set out on the lane. She was no longer surprised when it wound to the top of the wooded hill and the house whose every feature was now so familiar to her. The old man responded to her impatient summons. "Tell me," she began, "is this little house for sale?" "That it is," said the man, "but I would scarcely advise you to buy it. You see, young lady, this house is haunted!" "Haunted," echoed the girl. "For heaven's sake, by whom?" "By you," said the old man, and softly closed the door.[6]

5

Such a tale suggests how the imagination can move from reality to dream and from dream into a further reality. This concentration on dreaming or idealizing from pretended or spurious levels of reality found in tall tales and gossip to the shadow image of the dreamer seeing himself in a frightening event, unsure of being dead or alive, creates a bridge to the extended mediating level in the pre-conscious of the Epos, where, in a social sense, the group members are watching themselves reflected in a heightened world of social values. In the way I am using it here, Epos is the common dream of the nation or race where its fortunes are mirrored.

In his study of the hero, misleading as it may be in some respects, Lord Raglan presented a list of the characteristics in the cultural hero that we may still find useful, the overall pattern consisting of twenty-two major points, ranging from his mother's virginity, through the threat to kill him, his growing up in a far country, his eventual return and victory, his successful leadership, eventual loss of favor, and death. We remember that in this scheme Oedipus scores 21 points, Theseus 20, Romulus 18, Dionysus 19, Joseph 12, Moses 20, Sigurd 11, Watu Gunung 18, Arthur 19, and Robin Hood 13, and so on, whether these heroes come through to us in epic, romance, or ballad.[7] In his Hero with a Thousand Faces, Joseph Campbell further developed a study of their careers.[8] In earlier cultures the hero may appear as a warrior, a role hardly so popular now, in the later twentieth century, as it used to be. But the hero may still appear as the lover, a role more interesting to us. The roles of emperor and tyrant have little appeal to more democratically minded societies; on the spiritual level, however, the hero may appear as a saint or a redeemer, a role now assuming more popular importance at a time when the apocalyptic vision is engaging more people's attention, the saint and redeemer taking us into the deepest reaches of this sort of creative activity, encompassing ideal behavior from the most worldly to the most unworldly. In this regard, the Epos level in general is the mediating ground between conscious, ordinary activity and idealized patterns remote from historical conditions, where time relationships become less significant than spiritual beliefs.

In the structuring of these heroes' lives, the narratives fall into the familiar cyclic configuration, where such brief arcs of storytelling like the tall tale and the ghostly story have been displaced by

several interlocking arcs of events that pattern out
the departure and return, which Northrop Frye recently
developed in The Secular Scripture. He sees this
cyclic structure as the epic of man's eternal quest,
running from Homeric epics to modern science fiction,
all of which are derived from the folktale.[9] Also we
might recall, incidentally, that adult literary fantasy, from William Morris through Lord Dunsany to J. R.
R. Tolkien, tends to be based on the quest motif of the
fairy tale or Märchen. But, as Bruno Bettleheim maintains, although the fairy tale takes place in a never-
never land, its conclusion must be happy in a practical
psychological way so that the young cannot only accept
the chaos of their own unconscious conflicts but also
can hope to deal constructively with their emotions:
"Cinderella" lets the child know that a parent jealous
of a child's success should be punished, and "Jack and
the Beanstalk" gives the child courage to free himself
from parents and, after great tasks and dangers, to
find both the wealth of the golden egg and the beauty
of the magic harp.[10] In short, the hero departs from
the everyday level of the Rhema, across a threshold
that exposes himself to oppositions, trials and errors,
yet at times being assisted by a wiser or a more experienced person, to reach finally his goal, involving
a reward that changes his fortunes or provides some
benefit to society, to which he returns. Now his world
of heroic discovery can be related to his former world.
The heroic adventure portrays the eternal circle of
movement, the narrative departure and return, or the
psychological descent and ascent of man--the upshot of
the whole adventure depending on the meaning that the
society can give to the hero as its accepted warrior,
governor, or saint.

In the epic form, however, within the Western
tradition, there is perhaps an even more interesting
quality in the way the narrative is structured because,
to give dramatic emphasis and importance to the value
of the hero's career, it is typical since the time of
Homer with his Iliad and Odyssey to begin the story of
the hero in medias res, in the middle of things, at
some point before an important climax, where much significance is held in suspense, and the object of plung-
ing into this exciting situation is to call the audience's attention to the values involved in the hero's
career. And after this part of the adventure is played
up to a point, we then have degrees of flashbacks,
accounting, again, for the importance of the diachronic,
time-place Rhema in terms of explaining the earlier

career of the hero and how he reached, stage by stage,
the significant episode with which we began. With
various degrees of complexity, we may take up the hero's
adventures in his forward progress to the end and ultimate meaning, through which he is elevated to being
recognized as the ideal warrior, chosen emperor, or
divine savior or some such role that he can play in the
culture accepting him as their social hero. This displacement of the normal chronology suggests the psychological displacement of attention from merely one event
after another characteristic of the Rhema level found
in the simple time sequences of the tall tale and the
ghost tale, moving through a short time span to a rather
sudden climax. With the epic hero in Western tradition
we are in a situation where the events of his life are
worked out much more dramatically, concentrating on
central points and playing freely with time and place,
rearranging and displacing them in our attention to
highlight the significance of the hero. While the
material of the Western epic reflects the everyday
world, it is heightened by this rearranged and concen-
trated structuring.

A striking contrast occurs in the Eastern epic
tradition, in which less importance is placed on external historical causes, like famine, drought, population
changes, or even family rivalry, to explain war and
conquest but, instead, much more dependence is placed
for the Oriental audience on observance or violation of
moral practices and ethical duties of the individual.
As a result, the setting of the Mahabharata soon becomes
an idyllic world blending reality and illusion.[11] Since
the Eastern epic in the Hindu tradition is concerned
with discovering the constant presence of the spiritual
within the historical experience, neither the Ramayana
nor the Mahabharata uses the dramatic structure of the
Western folk or art epic but unfolds gradually through
the disclosing of the self-revelation in which the hero
discovers his own dharma, his essential moral nature
uniting him with the universal Brahman to overcome the
illusion of time and space.[12]

Further, in African narrative traditions, the
Mwindo epic, from Banyanga, Congo Republic, provides
sharp contrast to the more tightly structured Western
epic in its combining of song, dance, dramatic performance and gestures with the narrative episodes, whose
central purpose is to unite the epic bard with his
group in a public ceremony involving gift-giving and
feasting as well as storytelling. Through this African

8

epic, the hero Mwindo's character develops from an irresponsible braggart to a responsible moderator of society, having karamo, which includes health, wisdom, and group harmony.13 In this psychological respect, the Mwindo epic resembles the North American cycle of tales from the Winnebago Indians, who with some epic sweep show the importance they place on the stages of evolution from rash immaturity to poised maturity in their "Trickster" figure, an aspect of the hero that we will later investigate more fully.

Representative of later treatments of the Western folk hero, and his accompanying villain, are the so-called "legends" combining verifiable history with popular imagination in the form of stories of individuals ususally in short prose versions and told in chronological sequence, missing the impressive elevation of the epic narrative. Among the myriad of such legends, Booker T. Washington reminded us of the floating motifs in the story of unusual courtesy told about George Washington, Robert E. Lee, and Sir William Gooch, Governor of Virginia:

> George Washington, . . . meeting a colored man in the road once, who politely lifted his hat, lifted his own in return. Some of his white friends who saw the incident criticized Washington for his action. In reply to their criticism George Washington said: "Do you suppose that I am going to permit a poor, ignorant colored man to be more polite than I am?"14

The same tendency to embroider history exists in the current tales of the folk history of Florida, which I collected from whites and blacks, all such local lore using subjects accepted unquestioningly as genuine history but often compounded of narrative motifs and types established in folk narratives for many centuries. They are genuine memorates, believed personal history.15

In American Indian lore, the account of the origins of the Hopi tribe's home in Arizona structures the legendary history of these peoples in the familiar pattern of the interplay of opposites, finally producing a spiral centering on their permanent residence. One of the most reliable studies of Hopi lore can be found in The Kachina Sash: A Native Model of the Hopi

World by Edwin Wade and David Evans. The special cen-
trality of the Hopi universe is well documented by
seven Hopi informants of various clans, who all agree
on the Hopi origin myth of their emerging into their
fourth world. The four emergences should probably be
understood as expansions, for the end of each world
followed a punishment causing the previous wicked world
to be destroyed by contracting until it collapsed in
upon itself. Spider Woman always saved the righteous
Hopis, who were led to their next world. Although
Spider Woman dwells at the center of the universe, she
can extend herself to its outer limits, an excellent
instance of the dynamism in folk imagination between
the pivotal center and its periphery. In the natural
world surrounding the Hopi, the perfect metaphor for
expansion and contraction is the spider web.[16] In this
legendary account we already see the tendency to create
history as the mythic dynamism of polarities.

For the Mythos level of experience, it may be
futile to attempt to claim only one thematic content
as the monomyth, whether it be the narrative of creation in the eternal return of Mircea Eliade (1954),
Géza Róheim's death and apotheosis of the primal father
(1941), James Frazer's ritual celebrating the dying god
as defended by Lord Raglan (1936), or Joseph Campbell's
rite of passage in separation, initiation, and return,
first described by Arnold van Gennep (1909), as K. K.
Ruthven concludes in his study of myths and their
critics.[17] In this respect, we need to remember the
evidence of Franz Boas and Ruth Benedict that narrative
subjects and actions can flow from one sort of story
to another, with the result that "folktale motifs" are
found in legends and myths, while mythic and legendary
subjects are found in tales.[18]

In my opinion, the most satisfying treatments of
the Mythos level of imagination occur in the trilogy
of Alpha: Myths of Creation, The Wisdom of the Serpent: The Myths of Death, Rebirth, and Resurrection,
and The Two Hands of God: The Myths of Polarity. In
the first study, Alpha (Long, 1963), the narrative
structures of eternal opposites center on five major
kinds of methods: (1) Creation from Nothing, (2) Emergence Myths, (3) World Parent Myths, (4) Creation from
Chaos or from the Cosmic Egg, and (5) Earth-Diver
Myths. The dynamics of all such narratives exist in
the tension between what has been and what will be,
with the various mediating agencies or materials being
used to account for the transition to the state of the

world as mankind know it.[19] The Wisdom of the Serpent
(Henderson and Oakes, 1963) develops the psychological
response to death by showing the widespread tendency
in narratives to perceive death as a transition, not an
end, with death leading either to rebirth in a cyclic
view or to resurrection in a linear view. In this narrative context, death is the dynamic process of initiation into continuing experience on a fuller or a higher
level.[20] Finally, in The Two Hands of God (Watts,
1963), the narratives imply the hidden unity behind
the appearances of polarity, since the opposition of the
positive and negative powers, of a god or a devil, suggests the fluidity of experience never resting in either
extreme but revealing in their interplay the breadth
of experience from the illusion of many, which are only
after all phases of the one, so that mankind's ultimate
wisdom, esoteric and often taboo, lies in the vision of
narratives suggesting the truth of existence is its
paradoxical unity in the never-ending dance between the
good-evil, pleasure-pain, or life-death. The apparent
up-and-down of experience manifests the energy in this
game of life, where we learn to play as though the game
intended to choose sides or declare a winner because of
the ego-centered fear that the dark, downward side of
life, if given too much sway, might prevail over the
upward swing toward light. But the vibrating tension
includes all opposites and polarities, for all arcs of
the pendulum must finally make the inclusive circle.
As Watts concludes:

> In the light of this deeper and more
> inclusive sensitivity, it becomes sud-
> denly clear that things are joined
> together by the boundaries we ordinarily
> take to separate them, and are, indeed,
> definable as themselves only in terms
> of other things that differ from them.
> The cosmos is seen as a multi-dimensional
> network of crystals, each one containing
> the reflections of all others, and the
> reflections of all the others in those
> reflections . . . In the heart of each
> there shines, too, the single point of
> light that every one reflects from every
> other.[21]

When we reach this Mythos level of narrative, from
which moral meaning seems to arise not only in the
victory of the good or the treachery of the evil, when
experience may be seen either as comedy or tragedy, but

11

also in the vision of all contained in one, we may wish
to stop, for there seems to be no further extent of
storytelling we can talk about; the rest is silence.
Yet this apparent end of discursive experience can
mediate to further involvement, as Franz Kafka suggested
in his Parables:

> Now the Sirens have still more fatal
> weapons than their song, namely their
> silence. And though admittedly such a
> thing has never happened, still it is
> conceivable that someone might possibly
> have escaped from their singing; but
> from their silence certainly never.
> ("The Silence of the Sirens," in
> Imperial Messages: One Hundred Mod-
> ern Parables, ed. Howard Schwartz.
> New York: Avon Books, 1976, p. 5)

Kafka's remark leads us into the question of this
final level which I have called Logos, containing deeply
buried symbols that may motivate actions or arts in our
lives and have become embedded within the texture of
many narratives of the world that we have been examin-
ing. The myths, epics, and even more or less realistic
tales will have images carrying meanings from this deep
psychic level, representing a point of eternal return,
depending on the validity we feel in mankind's power to
recreate nature as a fundamental metaphor of unity and
harmony. Here we seem to be beyond time and place, in
non-discursive thought delivering us from the discur-
sions of myth, epic, and tale. The metaphors of meaning in the Logos may be susceptible to many degrees of
personal or social interpretation. Yet, in the sense
of transforming experience into basic symbols, there
have been as many poets among the folk as among the
writers of professional literature. "It is spectator
not life that art really mirrors," Oscar Wilde once
claimed. As a result, as we look into these stories,
there is no doubt that we may have certain connections
with them that the original storytellers did not have.
We can only approximate from the research of anthro-
pologists and folklorists what stories may have origi-
nally meant within their cultures. Still, it can be
shown that Oriental as well as Occidental thought can
structure experience in terms of binary oppositions or
polar extremities. For the Balinese, their landscape
and society represent more than a pseudo-Hegelian
thesis-antithesis-synthesis. In his study of Bali,
Miguel Covarrubias suggests precisely this kind of

internal and external structuring, dependent on the attitudes of the Balinese toward the geography of their island, where I observed the native life in 1971. The Balinese not only have made a unified metaphor of the complete island but also live with metaphors of each person's relationships to it. The controlling metaphor is known to them as their "Rose of the Winds."[22]

This unifying figure appears in the traditional method of planting rice on Bali, where each farmer, always starting with a pattern in the upper corner of his family plot, first plants a rice sprout as a central focus, followed by a sprout to the right, one towards himself (and the sea behind him), followed by sprouts to the left, upward toward the mountain in front of him, and four others to fill in the intermediate arcs:

9	5	6
4	1	2
8	3	7

In these cardinal points, the North of the island is always created by the invisible line joining each person to Gunung Agung, the great mountain, from whose waters the rice is irrigated, while the South is always the line between himself and the sea.

Although this plan appears to be a static configuration of established points, it holds within itself dynamic functions that condense the narratives of local life, for when the rice is pregnant, that is, after three months when the grain appears, a stylized human figure, constructed of palm leaves, showing a female with male genitals, is presented to the field to aid its pregnancy.

This bisexual union in the palm-leaf figure becomes the focus of the religious configuration that the Balinese imaginatively place like a transparent circle over the basic rice-planting pattern, for at the center now appears the hermaphrodite divinity, Siwa, followed by Brahma in the downward position toward the sea, this Southern region filled with the spirit of the creator-son of Siwa, and balanced by Vishnu in the upward position toward the mountain, this Northern region occupied with the spirit of Siwa's preserver-son. To the right is the clean area filled with the spirits known as

Pitara, the ancestors, and to the left is the unclean area of the Kala, the evil spirits.

Using their color conventions, the Balinese arbitrarily superimpose their color wheel in another invisible circle on their spiritualized landscape: Siwa, the All, is conceived as a mixture of colors, with red for Brahma at the South, black for Vishnu in the North, white for the right area of cleanliness, and yellow for the left area of uncleanliness. These cardinal colors are completed by the upper right arc of blue (between black and white), lower right of pink (between white and red), lower left of orange (between red and yellow), and upper left of green (between yellow and black).

All of these levels unite and become one to the Balinese, who represent the results of imbalance in their universe by the dance-drama in which Rangda, a creature of the Left containing darkness and illness, who was the unfaithful wife of Siwa and condemned to gloom and death so that she roams the cemetaries, constantly threatens to destroy the Balinese, who are protected by the lion-figure of the Barong, the male force of the Right having light and health. This life-death drama is assisted by entranced men wielding their krisses, the Balinese short swords. With the conquering of Rangda, the natives are free to pass their lives away from evil, to enjoy their rites and festivals almost daily until the final joy of release from the daily round to be returned as the cremated body in the ashes, purified by fire and then united with the currents of the sea, where the ashes are thrown, on the South shore, the final mediation from mortal land to immortal sea.

Under this unified multiple metaphor of life, the currents of sinister powers and black magic run, always endangering happiness; but, as one young Balinese man remarked to me, "We try to have nothing to do with all this for fear of unconscious corruption to ourselves once we open the door to these influences."

In this way, the Logos level of perceiving experience makes it possible for man to live imaginatively in a humanly constructed universe, in which the uneasy polar opposites typical of creation myths are overcome, the worldly heroisms of the epic are kept in place, and everyday events are felt as more than the seesaw of the superficial layers of accidental times and places, this Rhema layer alternating between the comic mood of wit

14

in the tall-tale exaggerations of climate, crops, hunting, fishing, and the like and the tragic mood of a
ghost-haunted existence threatening to destroy everyone.
Seen in this perspective, the folk narratives of the
world everywhere remind us to respect the composite
universal narratives that man has created to give
structure to his otherwise chaotic world as well as to
give direction to tensions within his own libido, as
Carl Jung suggested in his study of psychological
types.[23] Yet the drama must go on forever, as the
Balinese see it, since the enigmatic role of Siwa
remains as a kind of trickster, mediating, as Lévi-
Strauss says, between polar terms.[24] The trickster
contains the potentials of the Dionysian-Apollonian
powers present in the Hindu symbolism of the falcon and
the blood tide in the doomsday flood, central to Hindu
creation myths viewing life as the world-egg in a
closed system so that nothing is ever created from
nothing but instead each creation results from the
rearrangement of all, keeping in place heaven and earth,
male and female, and all other aspects of nature and
society, the Apollonian structure eternally working
through the Dionysian stream.[25] Long before Freud, the
Hindu imagination knew the power of Thanatos, as a
mediation from present confusions to regress to some
simpler stage, where all seemed in order, before the
apparent disintigration and differentiation occurred,
only to be displaced by the power of Eros as an emotion
seeming to unite us to each other but still seldom
realized and ending in less than perfect order. Forever, the philosophic elevation of the Apollonian unity
shown in the ocean of release from the world is contra-
dicted by the mythological conflict of the Dionysian
flame of humanity. Mythos and Logos in the world's
narratives exist in uneasy relations to each other,
since Penelope unravels at night what she weaves by
day. Still the Balinese vision remains the creative
challenge in mankind's story of itself, for the disintegration in the primal ashes allows the preliminary
step that mediates to another transformation since the
sea is not only the vessel of death but also the womb
of life.

To the Balinese the horizonal sweep of the sea,
where the ashes are strewn, is displaced by the vertical line of the pagoda, the synchronic symbol finally
overcoming the diachronic flow of the sea. For in the
pagoda the Balinese see the final consecration of each
person occurring in the ceremony of the mukur, when
each soul, now perceived as the blossom of the Rose

15

of the Winds, comes to its rest in the appropriate multi-
layered temple pagoda, the ultimate symbol of life's
story, after each has passed through the layered crema-
tion tower, which has prefigured in its mediating rite
the heavens of the pagoda, where most of the people see
themselves present in the low level of the pagoda,
closest to earth.[26] Here, in a kind of purgatory, they
enjoy most fully the life they had known on Bali. Death
mediates only joy for the Balinese as they pass through
fire and water to become guides and protectors of those
they love.

In such varied ways as I have shown, then, the
people of the world have tended to structure themselves
and their societies on the levels of the Rhema, the
Epos, the Mythos, and the Logos.

NOTES

[1] Alain Daniélou, Hindu Polytheism (New York:
Bollingen Foundation, No. 73, Random House, 1964), p.
231. Many cultural variations on the theme of the
point and the periphery in the circle are traced by
Georges Poulet in The Metamorphoses of the Circle (Baltimore: The Johns Hopkins Press, 1966).

[2] Zora Neale Hurston, Mules and Men (New York:
Harper and Row, 1970. Reprint of 1st ed., 1935), pp.
132-133.

[3] J. Russell Reaver, "From Reality to Fantasy:
Opening-Closing Formulas in the Structure of American
Tall Tales," Southern Folklore Quarterly, 36 (1972),
372.

[4] Reaver, pp. 373-374.

[5] C. Richard K. Lunt, Jones Tracy: Tall Tale Hero
From Mount Desert Island (Orono, Maine: Northeast
Folklore Society, 1968). Published as Volume X of
Northeast Folklore.

[6] Bennett A. Cerf, Famous Ghost Stories (New York:
Random House, 1944), p. 356.

[7] Fitzroy Richard Somerset Raglan, The Hero: A
Study in Tradition, Myth and Drama (New York: Vintage
Books, 1956), pp. 174-175.

8 Joseph Campbell, The Hero With a Thousand Faces (Princeton:, Princeton University Press, 1968), pp. 334-356.

9 Northrop Frye, The Secular Scripture: A Study of the Structure of Romance (Cambridge, Massachusetts: Harvard University Press, 1976).

10 Bruno Bettleheim, The Uses of Enchantment: The Meaning and Importance of Fairy Tales (New York: Alfred A. Knopf, 1976).

11 Mahabharata. Trans. William Buck (Berkeley: University of California Press, 1973), pp. xv-xix.

12 Mahabharata, p. xviii.

13 The Mwindo Epic. Trans. and ed. Daniel Biebuyck and Kahombo C. Mateene (Berkeley: University of California Press, 1969).

14 Booker T. Washington, Up From Slavery (Garden City, New York: Doubleday, Doran and Company, 1900, 1901), pp. 101-102.

15 J. Russell Reaver, "Folk History from North Florida," Southern Folklore Quarterly, 32 (1968), 7-16.

16 See the explanation of symbolism in "The Kachina Sash: A Native Model of the Hopi World," Western Folklore, 32 (1973), 13.

17 K. K. Ruthven, Myth (London: Methuen and Company, Ltd., 1976), pp. 75-76.

18 G. S. Kirk, The Nature of Greek Myths (Baltimore: Penguin Books, 1974), pp. 30-37.

19 Charles H. Long, Alpha: The Myths of Creation (New York: George Braziller, 1963).

20 Joseph L. Henderson and Maude Oaks, The Wisdom of the Serpent: The Myths of Death, Rebirth, and Resurrection (New York: George Braziller, 1963).

21 Alan T. Watts, The Two Hands of God: The Myths of Polarity (New York: George Braziller, 1963), p. 235.

22 Miguel Covarrubias, Island of Bali (New York: Alfred A. Knopf, 1937; 1965), p. 296.

[23] Carl G. Jung, Psychological Types (Princeton: Princeton University Press, Bollingen Series, XX, 1976), pp. 207-208.

[24] Claude Lévi-Strauss, Structural Anthropology (New York: Anchor Books, 1967), p. 223.

[25] Wendy Doniger O'Flaherty, Hindu Myths (Baltimore: Penguin Books, 1975), pp. 12-13.

[26] Covarrubias, p. 384. For further insights into the dynamic process of mythic transitions, see John Bierhorst's summaries of the typical varieties of transitions, or threshold crossings, in his edition of American Indian myths, The Red Swan (New York: Farrar, Straus and Giroux, 1976), pp. 22-25. Mythic transitions may be both positive and negative, fair and foul, according to Bierhorst.

As my study will show, these transitions involve the emergence from unconsciousness to consciousness or the experience that love provides beyond youthful innocence. Such personal maturing is reflected on a larger scale by transformations from animality into humanity or progressions from nature to culture, all of which may be subsumed under the inclusive concept of order being created from chaos.

A final transition from age through death to a rebirth and a new beginning runs counter to the other movements, which emphasize growth and maturity. This possibility of the return to youth raises the question of the values in unconsciousness, innocence, animality, nature, and chaos, which are on the side of youth.

The defeat of the vision for the Sioux Indians appears in John G. Neihardt's Black Elk Speaks (New York: Pocket Books, Simon and Schuster, 1932; 1959. First Pocket Book edition, 1972). After the butchering of his people by American soldiers at Wounded Knee, Black Elk sums up the Logos of his dream in his prayer to the Grandfather, Great Spirit: "From the west, you have given me the cup of living water and the sacred bow, the power to make live and to destroy. You have given me a sacred wine and the herb from where the white giant lives--the cleansing power and the healing. The daybreak star and the pipe, you have given from the east, and from the south, the nation's sacred hoop and the tree that was to bloom. To the center of the world you have taken me and showed the goodness and the beauty

and the strangeness of the greening earth, the only
mother--and there the spirit shapes of things, as they
should be, you have shown to me and I have seen. At
the center of this sacred hoop you have said that I
should make the tree bloom" (pp. 232-233).

CHAPTER 2

STRUCTURE IN THE ZODIAC: THE GROWTH OF

GARDNER'S GRENDEL FROM MONSTER TO MAN

I

The levels of oral narrative can be further understood if we put them in the context of contemporary
speculations about the levels of the human brain. One
of the most significant recent studies of brain structure is Carl Sagan's The Dragons of Eden (New York:
Random House, 1977). Sagan maintains that every human
being retains the areas within the brain evolved through
long periods of development. These areas, he suggests,
may account for the various aspects of human creativity
shared by the arts and sciences, united in their visions
of significant structure. The earliest brain development occurred in the "R-complex," which we still share
with our reptilian forebears. In this area, we retain
our sense of ritual and social hierarchies, realized
instinctively and not yet verbalized. A basic need of
the R-complex appears to be this enactment or realization of traditional order, which we become aware of in
symbolic transformations. The transitional area within
brain structure, the "limbic system," Sagan claims,
accounts for extensively localized altruistic, emotional, and religious qualities in our lives: here is
the function accounting for love. This expression of
humanity we share with our nonprimate mammalian forebears (and perhaps birds), Sagan thinks. The third
area accounts for reason being added to ritual and emotion in the "neocortex," the most recently developed
region, shared with some higher primates and cetaceans
like dolphins and whales. The neocortex handles reasoned structures of both nonverbal and verbal materials,
including such abstractions as the parts of speech in
grammar and human symbolic language. In this triune-
brain model, the neocortex, then, is in the position
of directing or expressing the ritualistic and socially
inherited strictures and orders of experience in the
R-complex and the emotionally charged ethics and incli-
nations of the limbic system. Richard Restak further
confirms these brain functions in The Brain: The Last
Frontier (Garden City, N. Y.: Doubleday and Company,
1979).

Sagan's view of the interrelated activities of the
biological functions within the brain suggests a corre-

lation with the psychological activities and their prod-
ucts that I have suggested for literary experiences.
The R-complex, beyond reasoned consciousness, still
functions in our need for ritualistic repetitions and
archetypal order. When this deepest, most primitive
area has been given a "word," a name or symbol, from
the verbal capacity of the neocortex, we label it the
level of the "Logos;" but the R-complex, in its often
remote, wordless silences, is still performing as it did
in our remote ancestors. Much of our actual behavior,
Sagan says, can be described as reptilian in our bureau-
cratic and political activities, although much communication in such rituals as a political convention or a
Supreme Court meeting is verbal and therefore neocorti-
cal. The elementary needs of the R-complex may become
verbal but their roots are in the rites and rituals
playing their roles in the primitive brain.

     The emphases in literary structures known in the
Western world as Mythos and Epos appear to be functions
of the more pre-conscious area of the limbic system,
where our humane emotions like the ethics of myths
expressing religious feelings and the noble, heroic
qualities of epics become the compelling motivations for
such structures, which we "feel" are right when we share
the emotional values, which have been given fuller verbal extensions than the ritual patterns and archetypal
form of the Logos.

     From the neocortex, the emphasis shifts to more
attention given to the importance in time and place,
the rational knowledge of history and geography, as
well as the relations of cause and effect, typical of
the more conscious, deliberate level of the Rhema, where
civilization is often correlated with the use of reason.

     In modern fiction, John Gardner's Grendel offers
a fascinating exploration of a creature that begins to
evolve through its disturbing responses to activities
typical of Sagan's R-complex and limbic system of the
brain toward the beginnings of rational thought and
poetic insight until he catches a glimpse of what it
may mean to be human. Grendel's responses, often ago-
nized and confused, to the human society at Hrothgar's
court depend on an ability to experience the levels of
the Logos, Mythos, and Epos among the people engaged
in the politics, wars, religion, poetry, and history of
the humanity around him. To give further implications
of the psychological development in Grendel, Gardner
has used the traditional signs of the zodiac as an

21

evolving structure through which Grendel experiences his psychic levels of growth.

II

In the October, 1976, issue of PMLA, Cary Nelson challenges critics "to re-create themselves and their readers in the otherness of a text they cannot claim as their own."[1] This kind of critical effort must be, according to Nelson, "engaged but disinterested."[2] When a critic attempts to interpret John Gardner's recent novel Grendel (New York: Ballantine, 1971), he is partly guided in his search for meaning by Gardner's hint concerning the structure of his novel, for he said that, through the voice of the monster, he "wanted to go through the main ideas of Western civilization . . . and see what I could do, see if I could break out."[3] In his effort at a sort of revelation for modern man, Gardner, who sees faith and despair as "the two mighty adversaries,"[4] offers his reader the stages of Grendel's growth in twelve chapters, "hooked," he says, "to astrological signs"[5] that give him clues to following the responses of the monster-persona, beginning to perceive "ideas which have been around from Homer's time to John Updike's time."[6]

Faced with twentieth-century ambiguities in self and society, Gardner appears to regard his position as a novelist somewhat in the same way that Saul Bellow does when he confesses that modern life presents more serious threats than Wordsworth's warning about laying waste our powers by getting and spending. Much worse than these, Bellow feels, are "modern distraction, worldwide irrationality, and madness,"[7] which threaten existence. Without offering advice to other writers, Bellow concludes, "I can only say, speaking for myself, that the Heraclitean listening to the essence of things becomes more and more important."[8]

Faced with dilemmas similar to those within the contemporary novelist, the critic of John Gardner has at least two guides toward some valid interpretive reading of Gardner's fiction in Grendel: the twelve signs of the zodiac and the Anglo-Saxon literature echoed in the novel. With these historical perspectives, the present interpretation of Grendel depends on accumulated associations with the zodiac together with Anglo-Saxon poetry having some plausible parallels to central scenes and concepts in Gardner's novel, seen from his view that it is a particularly "lyrical"[9] form,

22

building to a vision of humanity depending on the "real mystical touch in me,"[10] as Gardner confesses.

In his remark about all of his fiction, Gardner places himself firmly against the destructive attitudes of a novelist like Thomas Pynchon, who in Gravity's Rainbow knows "only the pedantry of chemistry and phy- sics,"[11] Gardner believes. Especially in Grendel the implicit human values gradually grasped in the monster's experience reveal how fully Gardner believes that "all the worrying and whining we did in the last generation was futile and wrong-headed."[12] In Grendel the percep- tive reader can find proof of Gardner's faith in "Shel- ley's idea about the poet as the legislator for man- kind."[13] Gardner's dream of this sort of poet is "a sort of African shaman, a poet-priest."[14]

With the historical guidance of the contexts of the traditional meanings of the zodiac and the reflec- tions of Anglo-Saxon inheritance, the critic can try to re-create his responses to Gardner's Grendel as a reve- lation from a poet-priest. With such safeguards, the critic may hope to be faithful to the purpose of art as Gardner sees it: "to celebrate and to affirm."[15] Historical perspective as well as careful reading of a modern text is needed to do justice to Gardner's fic- tion. Such an effort can, with some conviction, assume the process of "necessary misreading" from the subjec- tive concerns of the critic who may still agree that "interpretation is always in fact literary history: an error which assumes a historical categorization and con- ceals its own historical status."[16]

III

In the structure of Grendel, then, John Gardner relies on the order of the zodiac to explore central concepts of social and psychological experience. The twelve chapters correspond to the zodical signs, which provide Gardner the opportunity to dramatize the involutive-evolutive progress of the monster Grendel as a sort of paradigm for the development from animality to humanity. In his use of this pattern he makes an ancient structure modern. Gardner's originality comes from his ability to enliven the old meanings in the groping consciousness of Grendel, from whose viewpoint the world of Beowulf is seen. This study offers the first close reading of the novel to show the intricate interplay between the theoretical meaning of the zodiac and the specific language by which Gardner makes his special sort of dramatic lyric from the old English epic.

Conventionally, the first half of the zodiac represents the turning more and more subjectively to degrees of self-discovery, an involution or introspection that is necessary for early psychological growth. The stages of life, compared with the seasons of the year, are suggested in the three months of spring, followed by the cycle of the three summer months. Gardner's chapters correspond to this traditional pattern, the first three chapters representing spring begin built around the signs of Aries, Taurus, and Gemini, while the next three chapters are composed on the basis of Cancer, Leo, and Virgo. Together, these six chapters reflect the involutive journey to subjective discovery. The remaining six chapters, in the set of Libra, Scorpio, and Sagittarius (autumn) and Capricorn, Aquarius, and Pisces (winter), present a contrast to the folding in upon the self in the opening involution, for they turn to an unfolding evolution toward organic complexity, depending on degrees of maturity that appreciate quality of experience above its mere quantity.

The life of Grendel presents a struggle both for the monster himself and for the modern reader who realizes how much of the monstrous still remains in man, how much short he comes of the ideal of being genuinely human. Gardner in his socio-psychic structuring of this novel draws the reader into more awareness of the distressing similarity between a monster of the sixth century and a man of the twentieth century. Unlike many of his contemporary novelists, Gardner takes the stance of a man having affirmative attitudes toward society: his interest in an apocalypse lies not in the first stage of destruction, like Pynchon, but in the second stage of creative renewal.

Chapter 1: Aries (Ram), the head, associated with fire, suggesting an urge to create or transform.

Although Grendel tries to drive the "old ram" away (p. 1), he will not move, and Grendel must face another season in the twelfth year of the war that seems "idiotic" to him. Grendel recognizes the world "surging" in the ram (p. 1), stirred both sexually and intellectually (in his "balls" and "brains") with the same unrest of spring that the ram always forgets but Grendel remembers. To Grendel, the ram is only mindless urge to "mount" anything near. The ram, utterly earthy, cannot be aware of time or place but can move only instinctively within them. But Grendel doesn't see himself as noble, either; he can only hate the evidence of the "budding trees" and "brattling birds" (p. 2) that offer evidence of the passing of "seasons that never were meant to be observed." To observe such trivia is to be only a "poor old freak." And Grendel puts on a fake tragicomic show at his foolish observance of the silly seasons. He remembers with disgust the places among the spring flowers where he killed and ate his human victims and he despises the sun and trees that have observed his slaughter. Yet he senses the happiness of the deer that can "see all life without observing it" (p. 3). Grendel can understand that he is between creatures buried in mud and man, whom he is not yet ready to discuss. He takes comfort in his own shadow, an image suggesting some depth of psychic make-up that Grendel now perceives only in a limited way, as he continues to spin his "web of words" between himself and all that is not self. Already, Grendel is unconsiously moving toward Anglo-Saxon poetry, often called a "web of words" in those times. Resenting the return of spring with his renewed growling for blood, he swims from his dark hole under the earth past the firesnakes, which he sees as "hot dark whalecocks" in his erotically fiery mood of lusty spring. Emerging into the outside world, Grendel feels the presence of Space; he senses an awareness of place in this irrevocable time as a kind of "final disease," a sensitivity to fated history that the ram remains oblivious to: being aware of his hideous potential for bloody destruction, he feels he could die and wants the dark chasms to crush him. Although he is scared of his own voice screaming for destruction, he is not fooled by inanimate nature that will not snatch him, unless, he says, "in a lunatic fit of religion, I jump." Grendel appears to have enough self-consciousness to sense that ending his life might have a "religious" quality, yet it would result only from lunacy, not from a defiance of a Christian sin or a reliance on a Stoic Renaissance virtue, which has not entered human beings of his time, either. He leers at nature that has missed destroying him. As he moves toward Hrothgar's hall, he remembers his pride in the caution of owls and the alarm of wolves that knew him in his youthful vigor when he was still "playing cat and mouse with the universe" (p. 5). Now he objectively observes the sickness of murderous lust in himself, while the stars seem to tease his wits "toward meaningful patterns that do not exist." No longer absorbed by his youthful vigor for power and destruction, Grendel

rejects the fleeting suggestion of any higher meaning;
yet he feels his mother must have something "human"
in her because she suffers from guilt, some forgotten
ancestral crime, although she cannot analyze her curse
and never wanted to have Grendel ask why they are here.
But the dragon, whom Grendel sees as no friend, later
revealed the truth, very unlike the notions of Hrothgar's people that their sins have caused them to be
punished by some god through the past eleven years of
Grendel's bloody raids. From Grendel's viewpoint, the
people are praying to mere sticks and stones because
of their silly theories about deliverance from him, the
theories that the dragon told him would "map out roads
through Hell" (p. 8). Grendel despises the people's
ridiculous gestures of repairing their hall and of
making funeral pyres on which they throw rings, swords
and helmets. Most revealing of Grendel's insensitivity
is his dismissal of their delusion that some lunatic
theory has caused them to have faces showing joy as they
burst out with their song.

In this opening chapter Grendel remains largely the
victim of emerging spring and his blood thirst that
comes with it. But his reliance on what appears to him
as some wisdom from the dragon creates a transitional
movement toward something beyond Grendel's instinctive
hunger. The image of the curled dragon, the cycle of
time, carries with it the wisdom of the adversary
against which Apollo, Cadmus, Perseus, and Siegfried
fought, as well as St. George in Christian tradition.
Coming from the Greek derkein (seeing), the dragon
appears at this point since it has unusual eyesight, or
insight, that makes it ironically appropriate to serve
as the guardian of temples and treasures. From the
dragon's effect on him, Grendel is losing some of his
limitations.

Chapter 2: Taurus (the Bull), the neck and throat,
associated with earth, suggesting undifferentiated magnetism.

Grendel sees himself enclosed in a "skin of words"
moving before himself as though he is a dragon "burning
his way through vines and fog" (p. 11). The dragon
becomes associated with the snakes guarding the pool's
surface since both are, from the viewpoint of Anglo-
Saxon speech, wyrms, worms, lowly creatures of earth:
Grendel remembers his youthful thrust upward through
the darkness of the cave, resembling a primitive psychic
source, a deep unconsciousness, until he passed the

26

guardian snakes and discovered the moonlight. As a
youngster within the cave, Grendel remotely sensed the
distances between himself and the shapes of creatures
surrounding him, most of which looked through him in
their indifference, while only his mother looked at him
because he was her creation. Among his remembrance of
things past, Grendel recalls his being lured from the
cave by the smell of a newborn calf, but, his lack of
caution making him catch his foot in a crack between
tree trunks, he remained for hours feeling sorry for
himself and his mother until he realized from the
mechanical charges of the wild bull trying to strike
him that he was alone in the universe where either he
was pushing the rest or they were pushing him: the universe was the interplay of the brute forces in the bull,
the magnetisms of undifferentiated power. Grendel could
now laugh at the blind charges of the bull, which
finally gave up and left. The next night Grendel first
saw men, who mistook him for an oaktree spirit that,
being in a period of transition, must eat pig or "pig-
smoke" (p. 20). The push and shove of the universe,
suggested in the bull's charge, became more complicated
because the men, thinking Grendel's cries of hunger were
angry threats, became more skillful enemies than the
bull as they hit him with arrows and javelins, from
which his mother rescued him. Since she lived behind
"walls of her unconsciousness," Grendel failed to make
her understand his awareness of the brutish objectivity
in the universe, where she is the unconscious brutish-
ness like the bull. Grendel now knew the world resisted
him and he resisted the world. The prime lesson of his
childhood came from the brute magnetism of the bull.
But this shock also led him to realize that he is not
what observes since he can now observe himself observing what he observes. Only much later will Grendel
learn deeper meaning in being pushed by opposing force
and in escaping from walls that imprison him.

Chapter 3: <u>Gemini (Twins), the arms and chest,
associated with air, suggesting creative synthesis</u>.

After the primeval urge of the ram in Chapter 1
and the magnetic charge of the bull in Chapter 2, the
ram associated with Grendel's maturity, the bull with
his youth, a synthesis of experiences occurs to some
degree in Chapter 3, completing the first triad in the
structure.

After he was full-grown, Grendel settled on
destroying Hrothgar since Grendel had learned the

27

schemes of Hrothgar's men to attack neighboring bands
even though Grendel at first thought they couldn't be
serious, for even wolves weren't so vicious. But after
listening to their drunken threats and seeing them kill
each other in their brawls or drive out a murderer that
Grendel tried to befriend, he at last determined he had
to eat them. The increasing wars among the men had
sickened Grendel when he realized that, since he could
understand their language, he must be related to them.
Grendel had also observed treachery and betrayal of
allies and their stealing of another group's gold or
sleeping with the others' wives and daughters. This
human behavior had continued many seasons, through
which Grendel kept watch on them, until Hrothgar had
established a federation of the strongest groups and
demanded tribute from the weaker so that his meadhall
was piled so high with shields, swords, helmets, and
gold that the people had to move to outbuildings.
Hrothgar's power took in all the world that Grendel
knew, while his people felled forests, killed game,
built their huts, and grew sheep and pigs that consumed
the grasses and roots of the countryside. They even
built boats to drive their combat farther.

When the Shaper, king of harpers, came to sing of
Hrothgar's deeds, he patched together such effective
pieces of old songs of glory and greatness that even
Grendel believed the "lies," the tall tales. The Shaper
made everything seem true and fine; the men had "gone
mad on art" (p. 36). Grendel can hardly live with the
clash of feeling that the Shaper's poetry has created
in him: he knows the cruelty but he has heard the
glory. Screaming in agony, he hears his cry come back
to him: Lost! The epic vision of the poetry has
stirred a need for an apocalyptic joy in Grendel. One
world after another is being lost in this bewildering
succession of truths and lies. Yet the visionary poetry
of the Shaper has given a creative synthesis to Hrothgar's people, and Grendel has been caught up in it.

In his early life, Grendel existed on the Rhema
level of the senses responding to the animals and human
beings experienced in his growing awareness of time
within space, but, with the coming of the Shaper, Grendel begins to identify with a larger vision that ideal-
izes heroic deeds giving a more timeless human unity
to a nation. Epic poetry is beginning to shape the
appearance of the world to Grendel, and he is also
beginning to discover psychic values in himself that he
had not suspected. As a result, this Epos level of

28

experience upsets him and dislodges his conceptions of
a meaningless, objective world.

Chapter 4: <u>Cancer (Crab), the breast and stomach</u>,
<u>associated with water, suggesting gestation and birth</u>.

With Chapter 4 Grendel moves in the Summer arc of
the cycle, with much changefulness involved, shiftings
to new beginnings, and fresh uncertainties. "The sun
backs away from the world like a crab and the days grow
shorter, the nights grow longer, more dark and dangerous" (p. 39). Grendel now is living in his present
maturity after the nearly twelve years of attacking
these men of Hrothgar, whose ways have been glorified
by the Shaper, although the moving tragic art of his
moral song owes its origins all to Grendel. Hrothgar's
desire to build a magnificent meadhall to honor his
Danes seems only midsummer madness to Grendel. Such
efforts are to him only flattery and illusion pulling
them into a vortex. Yet Grendel is swept along with a
feeling of Hrothgar's greatness, and he can't laugh at
his pretentious ambition. Grendel is ashamed of his
bloodthirsty ways. He retreats like a crab to escape
the lure of the harp (p. 41), yet his mind is filled
with conflicting images. In amazement, Grendel suspects that the Shaper's singing had changed the men so
that they have forgotten their slaughter and have become
friendly and peaceful. But at once an inner voice
questions this impression, and Grendel remains tormented
by doubts. One side of him remembers the old terror;
the other side believes the reshaping vision. Still
Grendel suspects that he has become infected with poetry
and pomposity, while he also knows that the Shaper
sings for pay and women's praise. In spite of all his
wordy debate with himself, the split between his <u>per-
sona</u> and <u>shadow</u>, and the contradictions he sees between
the loving young couples and the poor murdered men,
Grendel is drawn into the structuring of the universe
in the Shaper's song that he hears when he returns to
the meadhall; the Shaper now has left the Epos level
of heroic deeds for the Mythos level of creation, a
narrative based on the binary opposites of light and
dark, good and evil based on the "ancient feud between
two brothers" (p. 43). Grendel is exposed to an even
more intense structuring of experience that not only
unifies the social group but also touches a deep realm
of imagination in his psychic experience: he believes
from the Shaper's myth that he belongs to the dark side
of creation, the "race God cursed" (p. 43). Grendel
cries, grinding his fists into his eyes like a child,

while he grotesquely holds with an elbow the corpse of
the murdered man he is carrying, without being sure
whether they both are cursed or innocent, or whether
the god or the twin brothers ever lived. The seesaw,
crablike motion of Grendel's awareness has reached an
intense peak: approaching the Danes in their hall, he
tries to become their friend but they hack at him with
poisoned spears; then, wild with confusion, Grendel
swears at them, using human curses he doesn't understand
except he knows these words reject the gods. His
thoughts continue to boil in confusion, tilting from
rejection to acceptance of the mythic vision, one side
of him believing in the "mindless, mechanical bruteness
of things," the other side being lured by the Shaper's
"hopeful dreams" (p. 46). Grendel hopelessly is struggling with the hint of imagination in him, his desire
to mold the world closer to an ideal vision: he
finally yields to his feeling that, in spite of what
may be just the Shaper's trickery, he wants the dream
to be true, even if he himself had to be the outcast,
for then he would know his place, though the victim of
the rules of the "hideous fable" (p. 47). But, after
sleeping off this nightmare vision, Grendel deliberately
tries to make his mind a blank and feels himself sinking
toward the region of the dragon.[17] Briefly, Grendel's
imagination has been stirred by the epic and mythic
visions in the Shaper's songs; but he soon sinks back
to the familiar Rhema level of living each moment in
physical satisfaction. He remains a romantic adoles-
cent in having faith only in the intensity of the
immediate moment.

Chapter 5: <u>Leo (Lion), the heart and back, associated with fire, suggesting psychological individua-
tion, maturity, and establishing a willpower.</u>

This chapter structures both the center of the summer triad, being the focus of the three summer months,
and returns to the transforming quality of fire, in the
quaternary of fire, earth, air, and water. It is piv-
oted, then, to the transitions in Grendel's inner life,
which approaches a climax.

In the presence of the dragon, to whom he now
turns, Grendel responds to the fiery fierceness of the
beast: his red-gold tail, his gold and jewels turning
blood-color in the dragon-red lights as the monster
breaths air over its inner furnace, flames escaping
from its mouth when it speaks. Associations are strong
here with the "red-gild" of <u>Beowulf</u> (OS gold - OE geolu:

yellow = ME juel, cognate with OF juel, diminutive of
ju, game, related to ME jupartie, suggesting not only
a "jest" but also "dilemma," something in jeopardy.)
Further irony occurs in the vision of the blood running
on the jewels of Christ's cross in The Dream of the Rood
since this association may serve as a foreshadowing of
Caedmon in Gardner's treatment of the resurrection of
Grendel through poetry. Grendel is overwhelmed with
this dramatic power, this ancient source of knowledge;
he seems like a little boy before the elderly sage.
Grendel is afraid of the dragon as men are afraid of
Grendel, and the dragon teases him because he knows he
is scared enough to pee in his pants (p. 50). Only
when Grendel threatens to throw one of the dragon's
jewels at him, does the dragon stop laughing and warns
Grendel never to touch his possessions. Knowing Grendel's confusion and hearing him confess that he is
sorry the dragon feels so sick and tired of the world,
the dragon delights in letting Grendel sink into a hope-
less vacuum: Grendel senses how thoroughly the dragon
is "serpent to the core" (p. 53).[18] Then, to show off
his brilliance, the dragon speaks to Grendel in words
that make him appear to be an oracle, but he can present the world only as it appears to a materialist. Yet
the dragon has an advantage over Grendel since the
dragon can see the illusion of the Shaper clearly
focused against the dragon's perception of truth, or as
a god, ironically, the dragon is aware of time and
space, yet trapped in it, not beyond it. The dragon
prides himself in his ability to see all time and space
from his practical elevation, knowing the inexorable
movement from past to future without any freedom of
choice, which relieves all of responsibility: the
dragon with a kind of divine knowledge sees the future
as Grendel sees the past. Neither causes either. When
the dragon acts, he simply fulfills the future that he
knows. To the dragon, men are absurd because they try
to exert changes by using cause and effect relationships. The dragon sees the Shaper as the giver of
illusions when he tries to connect facts in logical
systems presented as art. Since the dragon perceives
truth only through the monstrous sweeps of time and
place in the fullest horizontal stretch of the Rhema
level, it cannot be "fooled" by the impression of
significant meaning expressed through the individual,
who sees himself as important because he is focusing
on a tiny space in a brief time. The dragon, then,
like every mechanical determinist, sees the individual
submerged in the general. In the weary cycles of the
years, the world passes from apocalypse to apocalypse

31

with no real change or improvement, according to the
dragon. When Grendel protests at the dragon's fatalism,
it justifies Grendel's attacks on men because such
destruction spurs these people to recognize their
mortality: brute existence like Grendel's spurs man
to define himself, for Grendel can "scare him to glory,"
says the dragon; for it's "all the same in the end,
matter and motion, simple or complex. No difference,
finally. Death, transfiguration. Ashes to ashes and
slime to slime, amen" (p. 62). The dragon remains
trapped in history as accidental process or life-force.
His best advice to Grendel becomes only the cheap pity
of being kind to idiots and the egotist greed of getting
and keeping wealth. Since mortal man is confined in a
material universe, his best way to use his place in time
is to accumulate material possessions. Although Grendel thinks the dragon may be lying, it is still a logical creature perfectly adjusted to the Rhema level of
ego consciousness in the physical sphere, as all such
limited knowledge is.

Chapter 6: <u>Virgo (Virgin), the bowels, associated</u>
<u>with the earth, suggesting intelligence</u>.

This chapter closes the experience of inward
searching for the self, of discovering psychic potentials for maturity, and of seeing the role the informed
imagination has in interpreting the events of growth.
At this pivotal point, thoughts pass, mystically, from
space to non-space, from time to timelessness. Only
imaginative intelligence can grasp this transitional
unity, the zenith of experience from a subjective viewpoint. This stage of growth sums up all that has pre-
ceded it and mediates to all that will follow; its
balance is the dynamic transition to completed growth,
full career, and psycho-social expression. The primordial energy may now pass from the sense of diversity to
unity in the adjustment to circumstances. The spirit
has now become fully involved in the world of forms,
where ideals are materialized and expressed.

The animal nature of Grendel has been confused from
using its impulses to extend its libido out to others
that have rejected his attempts at some emotional union,
and Grendel suffers from repulsed affection as his feelings are turned back on himself. From this psychological viewpoint, the early experiences of Grendel have
shown his Promethean powers defeated and turned to
satire; but he is reaching a crisis where he must begin,
in the manner of the Romantic searcher, to define the

inner search for a Self after nature and men have
deserted him, as Harold Bloom shows in "The Internaliza-
tion of Quest-Romance."[19]

As Grendel says, nothing and everything was changed
by his seeing the dragon, for he has heard one kind of
view of past and future, but he doesn't yet know what
the present is, the present where life occurs. Yet
from the dragon an aura of futility and doom pervades
Grendel's existence, inward and outward, "my scent and
the world's" (p. 65), as Grendel expresses it to himself. Most disturbing to Grendel is the "charm" that
the dragon has put on him: now no weapon can cut him.
This sense of being beyond physical harm puts a gap
between himself and men; Grendel feels his isolation.

Grendel recalls the first year of his war with
Hrothgar, when the Shaper's song enraged him because of
men's confidence in themselves: he despises the heroic
hope of human beings, believing in a benevolent God,
here in this kingdom where "heroes were brave and
virgins were virgins" (p. 67).

Now Grendel discovers his invulnerability to the
people's weapons. None of Hrothgar's men can harm him;
he seems to be beyond the powers of the material world,
which he can now use in any way he likes, such as biting
off his attacker's head and drinking his blood. His
power fills Grendel with glee.

With this proof of his advantage over Hrothgar's
men, Grendel begins his raids, filling him with "a
strange, unearthly joy" (p. 69). Knowing his command
of the situation, Grendel becomes aware of loneliness
as well as his elevation above nature:

> I had become something, as if
> born again. I had hung between possi-
> bilities before, between the cold
> truths I knew and the heart-sucking
> conjuring tricks of the Shaper; now
> that was passed: I was Grendel, Ruiner
> of Meadhalls, Wrecker of Kings!
> But also, as never before, I
> was alone. (p. 69)

He remembers his past, feels his present, but fears
his future. In spite of his physical control over men,
he suffers from the jolt of his psychic separation from
them: he had felt closer to them when they met as

fighters on more equal terms. Now his victory is empty. "I felt trapped," says Grendel, "as hollow as a rotten tree" (p. 70). He sees himself killing without contest in this meadhall that seems "to stretch for miles, out to the edges of time and space . . ." (p. 70). In this way Grendel knows he has reached a zenith of power over nature but also a nadir of individual meaning. Such power has emptied his actions of all significance except mechanical repetition; he is "a meaningless smudge in a universe dead as old wind over bones, abandoned except for the burnt-blood scent of the dragon" (p. 70), and he madly strikes out at the meaningless world.

Then he meets Unferth, who is a misguided hero to Grendel and is making the mistake through over-confidence of attacking Grendel, who knows of his sure defeat: "Sooner or later the harvest virgin will make her mistake in the haystack" (p. 73). The intelligent superiority of Unferth appears to be mere virginal naiveté to Grendel. For a time, Grendel makes a fool of Unferth by throwing a barrage of apples at him, making Unferth weep like "a poor miserable virgin" (p. 74).

When Unferth tracks Grendel to his cave, where he hopes to die a hero giving his life in battle with the monster, Grendel has a moment of sympathy with Unferth's lonely desperation since he feels the emptiness of his life if he can never prove he is an epic hero immortalized in song; but Grendel becomes confused when Unferth shifts his ground to one of personal meaning, beyond the praise of men, when Unferth says he is proving "inner heroism" (p. 76) by dying when only he, Grendel, and God will ever know the manner of his death. Grendel finds it difficult to grasp such an internalizing of value: he feels that he has been placed in this whole "shit-ass scene" (p. 77) because Unferth has such a ridiculous theory of value, in which the hero "sees values beyond what's possible" (p. 77): Unferth has an impossibly imaginative vision of the hero, knowing he will eventually fail but making "the whole struggle of humanity worthwhile" (p. 77). The virginal purity of Unferth's idealism remains beyond Grendel, who can only see that such an imaginative interpretation of death "breaks up the boredom" (p. 77). The cynic and the idealist remain precariously balanced at this point. Instead of killing him, Grendel carries Unferth back to the meadhall, depositing him outside. From then on, Unferth can only go through the motions of fighting Grendel, who always spares him, so that Unferth, filled with shame, remains "furiously jealous of the dead" (p. 78). Grendel believes he has conquered not only the opposing visions of poets (epic dreamers) and dragons (materialist cynics) but also the outrageously funny virtue of the harvest-virgin, for he will not rape his pure vision of heroism. At this point Grendel has reached as much of an internal view of himself as he is capable of finding.

Chapter 7: Libra (the balance scales), the kidneys, associated with air, suggesting equilibrium.

Since the static point closing Chapter 6 cannot be maintained forever, the reverse movement now begins. From personal involution, Grendel moves toward social evolution. The descending action will now be compensated with an ascending action: in a Platonic sense, the spirit has fallen into material existence and needs to be rescued by returning along the same way. Grendel's degree of "experience" must lead to a degree of "innocence," but an innocence now somewhat informed by the experience. Everywhere his animal limits are played off against man's potentials. Grendel's worldly cycle has been condensed into a year, the twelve-month cycle starting with March, the springtime of the Ram and the sun's increase. This movement is the zodiac of man's imagination expressed in terms of animal associations, which Grendel is too much animal to understand fully. As a symbol of a creature too bound to the senses, he resembles Blake's Urizen. He is still too much embedded in the material world to grasp its imaginative analogy: he is one of the animals on a world totem pole, so to speak, without seeing the transcendent significance; or he is, as it were, too much the vehicle of the expression to apprehend its tenor. The quantity of Grendel's experience or level reflects both its own quality and its transitional value between preceding and following levels, suggesting areas of height or depth as superior or inferior. Such a cyclic view implies a serial philosophy perceiving that everything occupies a position within space and time limited to its situation, but, instead of being narrowly deterministic, this view presents a destiny implying that each antecedent must cause each consequence. This higher wisdom, knowing that any situation must have ramifications not replaceable or arbitrary, escapes the dragon altogether and remains largely beyond Grendel's grasp. In his novel Grendel, John Gardner is revealing the imaginative metaphors with which to see "the totality, the connectedness" through the "real mystical touch"[20] in him.

The nihilistic dragon occupying the center of Grendel's experience has been somewhat repudiated already by the monster's ability to keep such nihilism at a distance from him when he feels his power over Unferth's virginal heroism. But Grendel must still discover, as much as he can, how to affirm life. Such redemption from the nihilist dragon can occur only by "acts of imagination,"[21] Gardner believes.

Even the vision of the Shaper in his creating an epic heroism for Hrothgar's men must be surpassed. The level of the Epos does create a vision but, in the end, as Gardner says, "it's a lie" and its rationale must be left behind for a deeper truth. Grendel, in his remaining evolution, must learn how to be the successor to the Shaper.[22] "Poetry," according to Gardner, "is an accident, the novel says, but it's a great one. May it happen to all of us."[23]

Being sensitive to his uneasy balance during his brief control of the situation, Grendel can laugh at himself and Hrothgar because Grendel has enough artistic objectivity to realize that "form follows function," and if his function of being a Hrothgar-Wrecker ever stops he will have no form. Having no form, he will no longer be Grendel. Therefore he cannot destroy all of the kingdom: the indecisive balance is momentarily relieved by Grendel's appreciating its comedy in his kind of song, a serio-comic ditty:

> Pity poor Hrothgar,
> Grendel's foe!
> Pity poor Grendel,
> O, O, O! (p. 79)

Grendel shows what he is by what he considers funny. His introspection only confusing him, Grendel toys with being insane as he plays variations on his ditty, showing Grendel is crazy if he thinks Hrothgar makes it snow and, finally, by mixing the names of destroyer and victim in irrational balance:

> Pity poor Grengar,
> Hrothdel's foe!
> Down goes the whirlpool:
> Eek! No, no! (p. 80)

Midway through the twelfth year of his silly seige of Hrothgar's hall, Grendel speculates on the "holy number" of twelve, which somehow he senses must furnish his escape from this indecisive balance that has become his trap. Gardner allows us to see Grendel from an artistic distance for the first time in the novel as he gives us a glimpse of Grendel, battered and blood-stained, looking for omens and portents in the winter woods. Yet Grendel also looks on himself as another monster, a doppelgänger, who checks "Grendel's" mad search for meaning in a nearly schizoid condition. The impression that he is somehow watching himself act, and even talking about the way he talks, appears from the monster announcing "Grendel's law": "There is no limit to desire but desire's needs" (p. 80). Grendel is tormented by being a creature of instinctive desire who must curb his desire to prevent his extinction if he yields to his impulse to kill beyond his quota for the season. Grendel continues to take stock of himself as he senses this transitional time in which zenith appears to be nadir, the whole world somehow upside-down, with the devil standing on his head as in Dante's "Inferno." Grendel can pride himself on his round teeth, his safe cave roof, and his resistance to killing the queen, his ultimate act of nihilism, although he smells the dragon's scent heavy around himself. Grendel projects his odd transitional psychic geometry onto the queen's body, trying to see her, in spite of her "radiance," as a "surface generated, more or less, by the revolutions of a conic about an axis lying in its plane, and the solid thus enclosed" (p. 81). Wealtheow, the queen, somehow looks to Grendel like a "Time-Space cross-section" (p. 81) as he remembers how her beauty had upset him when a rival king presented her to Hrothgar, for Grendel was torn between Hrothgar's stupidity of granting a truce for the exchange of this woman and the adoration Grendel felt for her beauty, almost leading him to drool at her feet. For the first time the independent masculinity in Grendel is touched by the childlike femininity in Wealtheow, suggesting the emotional Shadow nature of his anima that he both hates and loves. For the first time, Grendel gets some inkling of the androgyny within himself. The queen's presence prevents Grendel from attacking Hrothgar: he feels she acts as a charm protecting the meadhall, and his male superiority is restless and enraged by being so frustrated. He is so disturbed that even his mother, in her mindless love, wants to give her own life to end his suffering.

The appearance of a new quality in experience comes from Grendel perceiving the change in the Shaper's music, now not occupied with glory and conquest but with the presence of "beauty that made time's flow seem illusory"

(p. 88). The Shaper can now sing of the humanity in beauty and comfort, something more permanent and softer than Hrothgar's raids, "heroic" as they might be. The court is held in suspense, resembling Grendel's own uneasy balance. It is the queen's childlike innocence that most affects Grendel when he can see how her glance, "Looking out from another world and time," (p. 89) made Unferth, a brother-killer, ashamed of himself.

Grendel, further, is touched by the sympathy between the old king and young queen when he sees her with her husband in her arms, holding "the naked, bony king as if her were a child" (p. 90), and by the loneliness Grendel can understand when he sees her leave the hall late at night to brood on her sorrow. But he is also stirred when he observes her happiness while she fills the mead cups during a visit from her brother, Hrothgar being filled with love and pride, so that Grendel feels never until this moment "had the old man been absolutely happy" (p. 91). Gradually, Grendel and Hrothgar are approaching a unity where the dividing line between monster and man is beginning to disappear. All of the emotional sympathies begin to be "teased toward a disbelief in the dragon's truths" (p. 93), and Grendel feels the pressures of his unexpected evolution:

> How many times must a creature be dragged
> down the same ridiculous road? The Shap-
> er's lies, the hero's self-delusion, now
> this: the idea of a queen! (p. 93)

When, in desperation, Grendel strikes at the occupants of the meadhall, as though he must set the record straight, he nearly burns the queen over the fire to prove he can "teach them reality" (p. 94) but changes his mind; for he realizes killing her would be "mere pointless pleasure" (p. 94) and no proof of order or meaning. By taking this stand, Grendel believes he has destroyed another theory, has shown that there is nothing in "meaning as quality of life" since everything is but a "frail, foolish flicker-flash in the long dull fall of eternity" (p. 94). Taking comfort in his memory of the bleeding ugliness between the queen's legs, Grendel convinces himself that he is cured of belief in friendship and love, although, alone in his cave at night, he still has to admit he is of two minds, hanging balanced between love and hate for the queen. Tormented by her beauty, Grendel alternates between killing himself and changing his mind, while he is helplessly "sliding down slime" (p. 95) toward an evolution he cannot be aware of. In such a situation, suicide lacks nobility.

As the novel becomes increasingly concerned with Grendel's private stresses, it leaves the episodes of external narrative to evolve into a lyrical expression held in suspense as the wheels of Grendel's fortune spin between his meeting the dragon and his encounter with Beowulf, as Gardner has suggested.[24]

Grendel's sense of balance always becoming unbalanced indicates that some breakup must occur. The balancing scales of Chapter 7 slide off into the disintegration of Chapter 8 since a kind of chaos must be reached before a new order can be made, the chaos here resembling the protohyle of the alchemists, the soul of the world, embracing all opposing forces.

Chapter 8: Scorpio (Scorpion), the loins, associated with water, suggesting the flowing away of forms, the disintegration of organic structures.

This chapter represents the transitional experience between the balance of Libra and the synthesis of Sagittarius as it is Chapter 8 in the triad of Chapters 7, 8, and 9, belonging metaphorically to the Fall season of Grendel's evolution, his necessary turning little by little to some integration with nature and humanity: this section produces the chaos that is destructive and creative. In both Platonic and Hindu traditions, as well as in medieval alchemy, chaos is seen as the soul of the world. Embracing all opposites within it, chaos represents undifferentiated dissolution, from whose potentiality creation arises. Psychologically, this primordial state may be understood as the black realm of the unconscious, the alchemic massa confusa of prime matter and thought from which the lapis may rise. Gardner shows how Grendel can catch at least some glimpse of this sacred stone within the darkness of his life.

Grendel finds himself "anger's child, red eyes hidden in the dark of verbs" (p. 97) since his speech becomes chaotic when he tries to express the shifts and changes he observes in himself and others. Confusedly, he remembers scenes like the arrival of Hrothulf at the Danish court after his father's death, the boy being a scorpion to upset the nobles, and Hrothulf's meditating on the violence that underlies the courtly order. The disturbed thoughts of Hrothulf flow in an intimate lyricism as he ponders over the law of the world, which he sees as "winter" and "casual" (p. 100), a place where stability can be established by something more than love (p. 101). Even the queen no longer feels her childish love.

Grendel welcomes the growing idea of violence in young Hrothulf, recognizing a kindred spirit in him, as Grendel overhears him talking to an old peasant man, his counselor, who encourages revolution by showing him that "total ruin of institutions and morals is an act of creation" (p. 102), an act of religious meaning, in which power is pitted against power (p. 104). When young Hrothulf protests at such violence, the peasant retreats into his belief that any system is evil: he will help him destroy the present government but doubts there is universal justice.

Yet all at court fear an approaching disaster, except Hrothgar, who has run out of schemes to maintain his power, now that he sees every effort at order only an invitation to disorder: strength, wealth, marriage bonds, all only give rise to jealousy and desire to possess another's advantage. He and Wealtheow are chained together in their trap, a peace never assured but maintained through ordeals with no security except their power until it fails. Seeing them in this predicament, Grendel needs no excuse for his hounding them, for he too is just another mechanical creature who has created Hrothgar's greatness and may destroy it as well. They are all raiders together, moving from chaos to chaos, monstrous energies moving against each other. In a sudden leap of fancy, Grendel creates a dream for Hrothgar, a nightmarish vision of two trees, grown into one, suddenly cut asunder by an iron blade. Darkness and destruction reign. In such a scene, Gardner's lyric temper has enhanced the original epic tone of Beowulf.

Chapter 9: Sagittarius (the Archer), the thighs, associated with fire, suggesting coordination and synthesis.

This chapter serves to culminate the third triad of the solar year, the zodiac of involvement and evolution through which Grendel passes, for Sagittarius, the centaur, expresses the complete man, at once animal and spiritual, linking earth and heaven, existing in the state of tension symbolized by the arc, or archer, shooting from a limited, horizontal base to a diagonal line beyond animal instinct to higher intelligence, as we will later see more fully in John Updike's The Cen-

taur. In this respect, Sagittarius achieves the state
of the scorpion men in Gilgamesh, where they are only
two-thirds divine. Associated with the month of December, this segment of growth also reflects the death of
the year to be reborn in spring, another necessary transition leading to ultimate fulfillment so that life is
not left in the mood of irony or satire, implying cold
rejection of the appearance of meaning in the earlier
seasons. Having passed through a spring of comedy, a
summer of romance, and an autumn of tragedy, Grendel
will now be tested by the satire of winter to discover
what values remain for him. He passes through the "way
of the dream . . . down and through it" (p. 109). His
imagination is caught by the impressions of "winged
creatures" (p. 109) left in the snow where children have
waved their arms across the drifts. They seem to suggest some ominous height or possibility of flight beyond
the mundane. Grendel senses in his winter mood that
"only the deepest religion can break through time," yet
somehow nature, like the barren trees, appears to have
some faith in the future (p. 109). Through Grendel's
groping feelings, Gardner is implying the opportunity
for continual growth from the "natural" to the "spiritual" along an ever shifting continuum of potentiality:
the animal can become man, man can become a divinity.

The riddle of the winter impresses Grendel even
more when he observes the dead hart, killed by Hrothgar's
bowman, lying in "the snow hurtling outward around him
to the hushed world's rim" (p. 110), a rim of space like
the edge of time at the year's end. The hart's antlers
had seemed to Grendel to be "like wings, filled with
otherworldly light" (p. 110), when he had seen the animal standing motionless beyond the hunter, who used his
arrow to reach the deadly communication with the animal.
In the movement, however, before the shooting, Grendel
becomes aware of the significance of time, held in man
and beast, each a chamber of an hourglass, neither able
to transfer sand to the other, neither able to reach
the other, until the world is reversed in its order,
since the time in them can no more be reversed in their
relationship "than sand in the lower chamber can rise
to the upper without a hand to turn stiff nature on its
head" (p. 110).

Grendel's burgeoning sensitivity becomes obsessed
with time as end and beginning, associated with the
sperm of the male that in its arc reaches the female
without a necessary spiritual context or value. Grendel
wrestles with the nagging suspicion that there is more

41

than the physical, which he has known mainly as over-
bearing force or destructive power. Symbolically, the
traditional arrow of Apollo and Diana signifying light
of supreme power in the sun's rays is being transformed
in Grendel's emotions into the phallus, striking at the
feminine center of life. The sperm's target proves the
conquering power of the male, and time's target reaches
its aim in the end of the year, both carrying the paradox of a beginning and an ending. In this sense, the
hunter by impregnating the deer has killed it. Grendel
is in the situation of the observer sensitive to objects
and actions but still confusedly groping for the imaginative meanings, twisted back and forth between egotistic coloring and more mature meaning. But he is on the
way in spite of himself.

Grendel's escape from the hankering after spiritual
significance comes when he can satirize the objects in
wood and stone in Hrothgar's hall where the priest prays
to the "Destroyer," the god of battle uppermost in these
men's minds. The Danes' god is like the Hebrews' god
of hosts, implored to defend the tribe. Since the
priests march in a circle before the images, Grendel
pokes fun at them because they may be "uncertain which
one is the Great Destroyer" (p. 111) among these powers.
Like Hrothulf's peasant adviser, Grendel is disgusted
with the killing of the calf, for it shows how these
warriors have degenerated from the good old days when
they sacrificed a virgin. Grendel sees their religion
as sick; no one believes in their songs, no one accepts
divine life in these sticks and stones. Grendel feels
he has discovered the truth when he sees Hrothgar and
Unferth, the old wise men, ignoring the images since
their "will to power resides among the stalactites of
the heart" (p. 112). Through such satire, Grendel
brings the "heroes" down to his own level. He remembers
well that when he had once raided the hall, breaking
the wooden figures and toppling the stone ones, only the
priests minded: the people put the "gods" back in place
just in case there might be something in the priests'
rhetorical wails. Grendel could not be bothered to
touch the images again; he only eats several priests.

Any aspiration seems to have hit the ground with a
dull thud, a comforting sound to Grendel, who has great
fun one night pretending to be "The Destroyer" hiding
among the images and shocking the priest by answering
him when he inquires who is there. Half believing he
has heard the god's voice, the priest claims special
knowledge of the god, and Grendel solemnly answers, "We

are pleased with you Ork," (p. 113), then teases the
priest to have him tell what he knows of the King of
the Gods, with the result that the priest, Ork, can
only stumble from one definition to another: the King
of the Gods is the irrational basis of reason; the
entity of multiplicity; the eternal urge of desire; and
finally the unity in the duality since "Time is per-
petual perishing, and being actual involves elimina-
tion" (p. 115). As beauty exists by contrast, discord
is fundamental to the universe, says Ork. Although he
is opposed by the established priests who fear for
their fortunes, Ork is adored by a new young priest who
seizes Ork's view of the Destroyer as the opportunity
to yield to uncontrolled passion:

> Both blood and sperm are explosive,
> irregular, feeling-pitched, messy--
> and inexplicably fascinating! They
> transcend! They leap the gap! (p.
> 118)

But neither the other priests nor Grendel can grasp
the emotional enthusiasm of this wild young priest's
vision; Grendel slumps back in fear that even "a monster's blood-lust can be stifled by such talk" (p. 118).

In the silence after the ecstatic outburst of the
young priest, Hrothgar and his court sleep through the
night, time stands still, Grendel hibernates from his
raids; yet he is restless, wanting to fall "through
time and space to the dragon" (p. 119), but he cannot.
He is only puzzled by seeing the sun with spiders
revolving around it when he looks at it from a tree limb
where he is hanging. Not yet ready for more than surface appearances, Grendel cannot see the spider as creative power weaving its web in a spiral converging on
the world's center, perhaps an illusion, perhaps the
Maya of nature, perhaps the destruction of phenomena,
created and destroyed as the spider weaves only to kill;
but also perhaps the continuous sacrifice that is man's
transmutation by which death winds up life's thread
only to spin a new one. The choice depends on the quality of imagination. Or, perhaps, since Grendel has not
found his language he cannot define himself. Unless he
can return to the dragon's sense of values, Grendel is
left with acedia. The reader having the religious
imagination that Grendel lacks can feel the opportunity
missed for understanding that the nature image, inter-
nalized, could have become a mandala holding Siva, the
creator-destroyer, at its center. At least for Grendel,

his life line and his psychic center have become extremely tangled.[25]

Chapter 10 : <u>Capricorn (the Goat), the knees, associated with earth, suggesting ascesis, rigorous training and self-discipline</u>.

Chapter 10 begins with Grendel's sense of torpor and apathy. "Tedium," he says, "is the worst pain" (p. 121). He feels himself the victim of having watched the seasons, of having become too aware of the passing of time: for him, to move from <u>acedia</u> to <u>ascesis</u> is more than playing with words. If he can grasp the significance of his static condition, he may move to another creative level. In this final triad of evolution, the transition is suggested by the Goat's duality: in the zodiacal sign, the figure has a goat's body ending in a fish's tail, implying the opposing tendencies of evolutive aspiration toward the heights or the involutive leap into the depths. In nature, the movements may be toward the mountain or into the sea. Here the Logos, as light and life, is simultaneously spiritual and material, the ultimate, inclusive metaphor beyond which is silence. As the "Word," it fights darkness and death, opposing evil and night. To think is to find the word; to become human, Grendel must discover a language.

Even the Shaper is sick while the people are unimpressed by the young priest's crying that the "<u>gods made this world for our joy</u>!" (p. 121). Without knowing why he feels so empty, Grendel senses some need for replacing the Shaper and his lies: only on the Logos level will he find some evidence of true divinity as the Shaper of life, the genuine creator. Meanwhile, Grendel can only play games with the goat, whose horns, pointing upward, try to ascend to Grendel's mere, his mountain pool. Although Grendel rolls boulders at him, the goat persists in climbing. Enraged by the stubborn goat, Grendel fells him by rolling a tree that knocks his feet from under him so that Grendel can hit him a couple of times before he can regain his balance: even then, the goat doesn't fall but picks his way toward Grendel. Although his skull is split, the goat climbs with his "great twisted horns" in the air. The goat is all upward striving while Grendel is all opposition to climbing. Finally Grendel kills the goat, and learns nothing but his power to destroy.

Opposed to the threat of the ascending goat are the depths of the sea: Grendel feels that the kingdom cannot be harmed as long as the sea remains filled with icebergs, but an old woman tells some children of "a giant across the sea" (p. 124) that has superhuman power, and she warns, "Someday he will come here" (p. 124); but, as far as Grendel is concerned, she tells only lies.

From this point on to the end of the Gardner-Grendel narrative, nature imitates art more and more, first negatively, then positively toward illumination. Grendel observes the courtly Shaper, now blind and filled with dreams, approaching death, with no comfort from his epic songs. The Shaper is beginning to circle back to his beginnings, reversing his sight and light in his time for blindness and darkness; his span of life, moving in space, passing through time, returns to its origins, the zodiac of his experience, his coming to Hrothgar's court and his going from it: the Shaper becomes his own stele, a two-faced gravemarker facing simultaneously in opposite directions.

When the Shaper dies, Grendel takes gleeful satisfaction in his decline to insignficance but finds his cave only a place of tedium, filled with his insane mother, tearing her fur from her own hide, a spectacle that turns his home into a prison where he tumbles, like an underground river, through darkness. Grendel is descending to his primordial depths, where he feels he has lost the sense of his own personal history, the Rhema of his adventures, as well as the ancient age of the mythic brothers' feud, the Mythos of humanity, having already relinquished any meaning the Shaper's courtly songs might have held in the shaping Epos for the Danish nation. Such losses, separating him from apparent relations to nature and society, provide a psychic discipline for Grendel, pained from the solitude he now feels. He, too, seems to be approaching the end of a cycle. "Back there in Time," he feels, "is an allusion in language" (p. 128); now, with Time lost, nothing exists. Grendel experiences his suspension in his Now, the rest of Time being only words, having no meaningful reference except to what used to be but is gone. Words refer to nothing now; for the Shaper, who rocked Grendel's heart with beauty and holiness, is dead, and Grendel's mother has died as far as he is concerned since there exists no longer the loving mother holding him softly in her arms. If Grendel has become conscious of himself through words, he is now losing

45

his consciousness, for his vocabulary has lost any significant relation to his own psychic, emotional being. In his low mood, Grendel can only regret that he failed to torment and wound the Shaper as much as he might have. "One evil deed missed," he thinks, "is a loss for all eternity" (p. 128). In his paranoic state, Grendel boosts his ego briefly by imagining more megalomanic grandeur that he could have achieved. Feeling low, he must imagine himself as high as possible. Casting his mother aside, Grendel goes to the Shaper's funeral, where he hears the Shaper's young assistant sing the old man's song of Finn and the Danes. The funeral occurs in the time of Capricorn, an earthy period, when all seems to return to the earth, a flat plane of existence with no mountain peak and no flowing sea. Time has come to a stop. "Abandoned," thinks Grendel.

But, shortly afterward, Grendel awakes from sleep imagining he hears "the goat still pecking at the cliffwall, climbing to the mere. Something groans, far out at sea" (p. 130). Dynamic urges are still at play. When his mother groans, Grendel has a flash of warning through his mind: "Beware the fish." Subconsciously, he is being stirred by this archetypal image, the complement of the goat in the sign of Capricorn: the fish, however, may suggest here, beyond being one half of the goat-fish image, the cosmic fish, the symbol of progress through the world across the sea of unformed realities or of worlds that have been dissolved. This potentiality in the metaphorical fish carries the weight of artistic meaning through its occurring to Grendel in the moment when his world has dissolved: he is nowhere in the history of the Rhema, the grandeur of the Epos, or the glory of the Mythos. But the Logos begins to appear in terms of the fish, the mediating metaphor, the psychic and mystic creature living in water, representing dissolution but also renovation. Grendel fears his own regeneration; his ego tells him to beware of the fish because it may draw him into realms of experience he is not prepared to face. If nature is to imitate art, if structure is to control narrative, if Grendel is to become more than he is, if the word is to become the thing, then the awareness of the fish must provide the transition from life, dissolved, shapeless, to life, resolved, shaped into new creative form.

Grendel can only wait for a new savior after his apocalypse, resting in the stasis of belief that nihil ex nihilo. Death and destruction still seem the only

realities when he awakes from his terrifying dream with
the feeling of hands on his throat.

Chapter 11: Aquarius (the Water Carrier), the
ankles, associated with air, suggesting illumination.

Grendel has now reached the apparent end of his
cycle: he knows the dragon was right; everything is
nothing. Yet the waters in which the threatening fish
lives persist in their flow into his life. In spite of
his animalistic, egotistic conclusions about his experience with man and nature, Grendel can be touched by
powers beyond his usual sense of strength. He finds
himself moving, metaphorically, into the arc of Aquarius,
which, in the Egyptian Zodiac, appears as a man pouring
water from two amphorae, the two streams of water being
the active and the passive aspects of its force, the
evolution and involution through which Grendel has been
passing. This waxing and waning of experience, for the
ancient Egyptians, was seen in the Nile, flooding the
land to produce new life for nature and man. Aquarius,
then, suggests the necessary dissolution of forms existing in any process or cycle and the coming imminence of
liberation and illumination.

When the sea waters become full of icebergs,
strangers come to the land in their "sea-eager" ships
(p. 133), bringing new fat men for Grendel's food: he
is filled with joy. Feeling their approach even while
he is still in his cave, Grendel is drawn to them as
he once had been drawn by the dragon. The beating of
his heart imitates the footsteps of the men. When Grendel reaches the shore, he sees a whale passing through
the dark sea, a shadow two miles away, without his yet
being conscious that the whale in those waters may be
there because, to many men, it is a mystic mandorla,
suggesting the intersection between the circles of
heaven and earth, embracing opposites of existence.
When Grendel sees the coastguard threaten the strangers'
leader, he rejoices in the promised destruction. But
the stranger answers mildly, with words having gentle
power, while Grendel notices how youthful he looks with
"no more beard than a fish" (p. 135). Without being
aware of himself, Grendel is making a connection between
this beardless seaman and the threatening fish of his
dream. To Grendel, this stranger must be some kind of
magician. The seaman, seeming like an outsider everywhere, speaks remotely about his people, the Geats, who
have come to visit Hrothgar, although he ironically
hints at some mission more important as though "he had

centuries" (p. 135) in which to accomplish his purpose,
which turns out to be the protecting of the Danes from
their enemy. Again, in spite of himself, Grendel nearly
falls into a trance as he gazes at the stranger's strong
shoulders. Even though Grendel knows this visitor has
come to kill him, Grendel is fascinated by his "sea-
pale eyes" (p. 136). This stranger seems half man,
half sea creature; half human, half wizard to Grendel.
In responding to this odd transitional character of
the stranger, Grendel is unconsciously preparing himself
for a mediating shift within his own values as a con-
tented monster in control of his circumstances. Yet,
when he returns to his cave, Grendel mysteriously
becomes aware of his surroundings: "I was unnaturally
conscious, for some reason," he says, "of the sounds
in the cave: the roar of the underground river hundreds
of feet below our rooms, reaming out walls, driving
deeper and deeper" (p. 137). This river, with the
seepage producing stalagmites and the spattering of
springwater in the distance, all haunt Grendel, who is
slowly, imperceptibly verging on an artist's consciousness of nature as a metaphor. The familiar waters seem
to convey something of a hidden meaning. In a kind of
creative daydream, between waking and sleeping, Grendel
begins to feel the peculiar condition of the creative
artist: "I felt as if I were myself the cave, my
thoughts coursing downward through my own strange hol-
lows . . . or some impulse older and darker than
thought, as old as the mindless mechanics of a bear,
the twilight meditations of a wolf, a tree. . ." (p.
137). Without knowing what it all means, Grendel is
gradually reaching his own creative depths where the
reviving flow of imagination moves. Nature is no longer
his adversary, his opponent, his sustenance, but has now
become the image of his own creative unconsciousness,
the inner river of his imaginative life. He knows only
that he feels a joyful excitement, while thinking
becomes unreal; he struggles with the "two great, dark
realities, the self and the world--the two snake-pits"
(p. 138) and draws an analogy, like a poet, between his
unexpected impulses and the dignified, disciplined
family man who impulsively slipped from his house to
spend the night with a hunter's wife. Was this act
only escape from tedium? Grendel wonders why the
"cavernous heart" suddenly strikes when the "watchful
mind" sleeps.

Escaping from his riddles, Grendel slips back into
a dragon-view of the world made up only of "things to
be murdered, and things that would hinder the murder of

things" (p. 139). When he reaches the meadhall, he is
pleased to see that the Danes are not happy to have the
Geats come to save them: their honor is threatened by
being bailed out by strangers; the priests are upset to
have their religion discounted since they always
preached that the Destroyer would take care of everything in due time. Grendel sees himself as the useful
instrument of the Danes' honor since religion is useless
to save them from their alternatives:

> Theology does not thrive in the world of
> action and reaction, change: it grows
> on calm, like the scum on a stagnant pool.
> And it flourishes, it prospers, on decline.
> Only in a world where everything is
> patently being lost can a priest stir
> men's hearts as a poet would by maintain-
> ing that nothing is in vain. For old
> times' sake, for the old priest's honor,
> I would have to kill the stranger. And
> for the honor of Hrothgar's thanes.
> (pp. 139-140)

Grendel brings himself to an encounter more perilous
than he knows.

Unferth now recognizes the strangers' leader as
the great swimmer, a man of the sea who had been in a
contest with Breca for seven nights, but had been
defeated; so Unferth boasts that the Geats could not
stand up to their monster, Grendel. But the stranger
replies that during the swimming contest he had killed
several sea monsters and really beat Breca since he
could not have won such battles, and neither could any
of the Danes. Hrothgar likes the challenge, although
Grendel thinks the stranger must be mad, but the king
is embarrassed when the queen appears and says she is
glad that at last she has found a man "whose courage
I can trust" (p. 143). Meanwhile, Grendel feels the
fear of this stranger's power, senses the changes he
might cause in him, yet reassures himself that he is
just as strong as this mild mannered man, and he begins
to think that perhaps Unferth has genuine heroism in
him, after all, not the mere rhetoric of the Shaper's
epics. Seeming to know a doomed people, the stranger
only smiles.

Grendel, vaguely aware of some moment of illumination, some salvation from the oppositions, waits while
the stranger also waits and the new young Shaper sings,

accompanied by the harp of the old dead Shaper, that they have only to wait while the frost falls and fair weather returns. All is left in silence and suspense. In what way will the water flow?

Chapter 12: <u>Pisces (the Fish), the feet, associated with water, suggesting mystic fusion</u>.

So far whenever Grednel has reached an apparent opportunity to transcend his limits, he has fallen back into his animal scepticism or the dragon's beguiling cynicism. Without his full awareness, however, Grendel has reached a mediating set of experiences that are propelling him toward the destruction of the old ways and the discovery of new ones. The quality of the transition in the arc of Pisces, closely associated with the properties of water, rests for Grendel mainly in the surge of cosmic energy implied in the oceans of the world, geographically and psychologically. While Capricorn has marked the preparatory dissolution of values, Pisces contains within its realm the origin of a new cycle, more maturely spiritual, the Omega and the Alpha of psychological process.

The symbolic fish has become identified with a kind of salvation and resurrection in the world's religions from the avatar of Vishnu to the emblem of Christ and forms a central creative potential in the figure of Oannes, the man-fish, in Chaldean myth. On the psychic plane, the tremendous ordeal of the individual must be felt as the agony of dying to the ego and the joy of waking to the self. The denial of destructive passions gives rise to the acceptance of creative impulses, now directed toward less selfish aims: the traditional mystic experience of losing all to gain all is achieved. The duality yet unity is effectively presented in the visual arrangement of the zodiacal sign, for it is composed of two fishes placed parallel to each other, but facing opposite directions, the left fish representing the involvement of the self in the world of nature and society, the right fish representing the evolution within the self so that it can rise beyond its limited circle. Ultimately the circle should become a continuous spiral of evolution. The structure of the novel <u>Grendel</u> must depend on the evolution of the monster Grendel.

The final chapter opens with Grendel gleefully bursting through the meadhall door, a passage into new adventures and the antithesis of the wall. Throughout

50

this final movement in Grendel's life, the culmination
of a kind of cyclic symphony, Grendel is confronted
with being included or excluded from significant developments for himself in his progress toward some degree
of emotional and psychological maturity: his life,
without his knowing it, has been a succession of doors
and walls. In his triumph now, Grendel fancies himself
already something of a poet when he feels that the
planks he tramples had "protected the hall like a hand
raised in horror to a terrified mouth" (p. 147). As
Grendel begins to eat the sleeping men, he becomes the
personification of devouring earth, consuming all in
sight, reducing all to a process of digestion, seeming
to prove that all end in death as he plays his role in
his limited view of an apocalypse. But a shock awaits
him, for one man is closely watching him and grasps
his hand with a grip like a dragon's jaws. Grendel has
suddenly shifted from being the subject of the action
to being its object; when he thought he was at the center, he finds he is only on the circumference. He is
so completely displaced that he feels the "long pale
dream, my history, falls away" (p. 148), and his opponent in the fight appears to have fiery wings, something
supernatural, but truer than the illusion of Grendel's
earlier life in the nature he knew. Yet, when he
believes his sanity has returned, Grendel sees the warrior as only a man, but a man who fights not only with
his arms but also with his words. After blacking out
from a fall, Grendel becomes conscious of his opponent's
syllables licking at him like "chilly fire" (p. 149),
in a confusion of images, all focusing on the death-
birth transition that Grendel has been pushed into:
now, "where the water was rigid there will be fish,"
Grendel hears. "The world will burn green, sperm
build up again" (p. 149). As he is about to be killed,
Grendel is told, "Time is the mind," the message of
this strange opponent who simultaneously promises death
and life, talk that Grendel still thinks is only
betrayal. But instead of appearing powerful, Grendel
becomes as a child again, crying "Mama!" and he seems
to be surrounded by vague shapes like seaweed. Grendel
will not accept "mind" from his enemy but protests
that his advantage was only "mindless chance." Unconsciously, Grendel is being dissolved in a sea-change.
He can only howl when he hears that the point of his
life is not whether he make it "a grave or a garden"
but that he now must feel the wall as he is slammed
into it. Hardness is all. "Observe the hardness,"
Grendel now hears. First, Grendel must know that he
has been trapped within the walls of a cave greater

51

than his cavern under the pool, to know his own impo-
tence and limits from which, as long as he remains
Grendel, he can never escape, although typically, when
he was with his mother, he felt the cavern walls as
protection from danger, his home as a mother's womb.
Like the Shulamite in the Song of Songs, Grendel must
appreciate the absurd wisdom claiming, "I am a wall,"
the wall being the feminine, inclosing, passive, and
material aspect of life, opposed to the masculine, free-
ing, active, and spiritual aspect: the house is but
the home of the spirit, and this false security must
be left for greater growth.

   The spirit in Grendel grows when he responds to
the command to sing: a larger will is forcing him
to realize his hidden capacity to break loose from his
captivity, like Jonah from the whale's belly, and so he
blindly sings of the hardness of walls. Still impri-
soned within his walls, Grendel sings the song of falling walls, perhaps still clinging to the hope that the
wall that injures him will fall, but echoing perhaps
the Anglo-Saxon view of the inevitability of fateful
destruction while time passes, as in "The Ruin":

>   Wondrous is this wall-stone; broken by
>   fate, the castles have decayed; the work
>   of giants is crumbling. Roofs are fallen,
>   ruinous are the towers, . . . Often this
>   wall, grey with lichen and stained with
>   red, unmoved under storms, has survived
>   kingdom after kingdom; its lofty gate
>   has fallen . . . the bold in spirit bound
>   the foundation wall wondrously together
>   with wires. . . . Fate the mighty over-
>   turned that. The wide walls fell. . . .[26]

Such admission of the falling of barriers in the past
satisfies Grendel's tormenter, but partially, for he
knows how far Grendel still has to move from terror to
joy. Gardner may be relying on the reader's memory of
the angel who appeared to Caedmon, in Bede's Ecclesiastical History, when Caedmon is told to sing but protests
his ignorance, which the angel ignores by telling him
to sing "the beginning of created things."[27] At least
Grendel returns to his beginnings, bawling like a baby,
while the opponent, a kind of angelic Beowulf, "stretches
his blinding white wings and breathes out fire" (p. 151)
as a new, redemptive dragon, but now more the final
image in Grendel's creative growth, an archetypal metaphor in his level of the Logos, from which unconscious

creative purposes are working. For Gardner, Beowulf is a Christ figure as a mediating power from paganism to Christianity and a redemptive power within Grendel himself, the force urging him across the barrier of separation from his deeper self, the wall dividing the physical from the spiritual. As among the Olympians, in Greek myth, Grendel goes through a transformation like that of Hermes, who adds to his chthonic serpent nature the attributes of birds: Hermes' staff acquires wings, and he becomes the winged man with winged hat and sandals. In a sense, by Grendel internalizing the winged figure that has been seeming to fight him, he has opened himself to a winged life, almost as though he has been subject to the trickster-savior in the Beowulf-Hermes figure as Gardner presents him. Whether only Beowulf, or Hermes, or Christ, the powerful stranger has led Grendel's spirit to a crossroad, and he is impelled to move on. Although his opponent may remain "crazy" to Grendel, he finds he must move to the edge of the cliff: no one follows him; he is propelled by some power in himself to cross the brink: "I seem to desire the fall," thinks Grendel, "and though I fight it with all my will I know in advance that I can't win" (p. 152). He feels "the dark power moving in me like an ocean current" (p. 152). Walls of resistance have fallen down; Grendel flows with a current of life larger than he had ever known, the power, to Grendel like a "dread night monarch" whose center is everywhere and whose circumference is nowhere. Grendel dies knowing he has had an accident, his kind of fortunate fall, a plunge into rebirth, which he hopes all may have. Grendel has begun to see "the whole universe: life and death, his own death. Poetry is an accident, the novel says, but it's a great one. May it happen to all of us."[28]

Sensing the selfless universality of his salvation, Grendel at last has had the vision of himself as part of all humanity and knows the agonizing joy of being human as he dies. This experience is the full extent of the modern apocalypse that interests Gardner: the revelation of the saving vision. Beyond the destruction, lies creation, the artistic insight that has made of Grendel, for a few moments, a new Shaper, who has vaguely felt another heroic vision.

Almost until his end, Grendel sees his opponent as an apocalyptic beast, the opposite to a savior, as still a snake or dragon, still a force of stagnation and death, preventing Grendel from continuing his lusty life. Ironically, the cynical dragon, Grendel's earlier

53

counselor, nearly wins in this self-satisfied, ego-
seeking side of experience. But Grendel had made the
mistake of seeing divinity in his own image. In spite
of his dragon sympathies and confusions, Grendel moves
beyond his monster nature in this encounter with Beowulf, who has created a new spirit in Grendel, fulfilled
the promise of the zodiac from the Ram of earthy spring
to the Fish of mystic unity, and completed the narrative of human experience as a transcendent structure
improving Grendel's lot, and mankind's, beyond any original expectation through the power of the transforming
word, the song of life that moves to a new spring, a
new region of a higher zodiac than modern man usually
knows. In spite of himself, Grendel has approached
the brink of humanity when he becomes his own Shaper
of song, creator of structured music.

NOTES

[1] Cary Nelson, "Reading Criticism," PMLA 91 (1976),
p. 813.

[2] Nelson, p. 813.

[3] Joe David Bellamy, The New Fiction: Interviews
with American Writers (Urbana: University of Illinois
Press, 1974), p. 173.

[4] Bellamy, p. 187.

[5] Bellamy, p. 174.

[6] Bellamy, p. 174.

[7] Saul Bellow, "A World Too Much With Us," Critical Inquiry, 2 (1975), p. 9.

[8] Bellow, p. 9.

[9] Bellamy, p. 186.

[10] Bellamy, p. 176.

[11] Bellamy, p. 184

[12] Bellamy, p. 184.

[13] Bellamy, p, 178.

[14] Bellamy, p. 178.

[15] Bellamy, p. 185.

[16] Jonathan Culler, "Beyond Interpretation: The Prospects of Contemporary Criticism," Comparative Literature, 28 (1976), p. 256.

[17] See Gardner's remark in Bellamy, p. 179: The Shaper creates a rationale of heroism for the people which is "a lie, but it's also a vision."

[18] Gardner calls the dragon "a materialist," Bellamy, p. 175.

[19] Yale Review, 58 (1969), reprinted in Harold Bloom, ed., Romanticism and Consciousness: Essays in Criticism (New York: W. W. Norton & Company, 1970), pp. 3-24.

[20] Bellamy, p. 176.

[21] Bellamy, p. 178.

[22] Bellamy, p. 179.

[23] Bellamy, p. 180.

[24] Bellamy, p. 186.

[25] For further insight into the intricacy of the language and the narrative in fiction, see J. Hillis Miller, "Ariadne's Thread: Repetition and the Narrative Line," Critical Inquiry, 3 (1976), pp. 57-77.

[26] R. K. Gordon, ed., Anglo-Saxon Poetry (London: J. M. Dent & Sons, 1962), p. 84.

[27] Bede, Ecclesiastical History of the English People, ed. James Campbell (New York: Washington Square Press, 1968), Book 4, Chapter 24, pp. 227-230. I am grateful to my colleague Dr. Allan P. Robb for the helpful conversations we had about the Anglo-Saxon backgrounds for the interpretation.

[28] Bellamy, p. 180.

CHAPTER III

THE SHAPE-SHIFTING TRICKSTER:

EVOLUTION TOWARD MATURITY

I

In The Treasures of Darkness Thorkild Jacobsen
reveals the social evolutions in ancient Mesopotamian
religion as they are revealed in the extant archeologi-
cal evidence containing much epic and mythic material.
The results of his study show how the Sumerians and
later inhabitants of Mesopotamia transformed the experiences of their daily social circumstances (the Rhema
of their lives) into structures of belief, which gradually declined as circumstances changed. Held within the
epic and mythic narratives, their archetypal animal
symbols, their heroes undergoing tests and trials, their
kinds of divine mothers and fathers, and their quests
through the underworld suggest, once again, the distilling of symbolic experience in the Logos level and the
reliance on ritual meaning and social hierarchies in
the basic brain that Sagan calls the R-complex.
Although the remaining texts date from only about 2000
B.C., they probably contain much more ancient subjects.

From this rich literature of the early Bronze age,
we can discover the processes of thought that produced
the evolution of social beliefs. In their relationships
with the numinous "Wholly Other" contained in their
religious metaphors, these peoples conceived of the
divine, according to Jacobsen, first, as a kind of élan
vital, the pervading divine powers in natural phemomena
having the will to direct and influence their economic
welfare; second, as the rulers of their society; and
third, as divine parents caring for the individual as
human parents do for their children.[1] The Mesopotamian
gods were at first bound within natural phenomena so
that they are "intransitive," in Jacobsen's term, like
the ancient nonhuman form of the lion-headed bird representing the roaring thundercloud. Following this kind
of metaphor, the image of the political ruler appears--
such as the "Lord Wind" with a kind of parliament of
gods reflecting later social developments. The more
"mythic" view of divinity within all nature, determining
life in general, starts to be made more socially specific when the more "epic" type of hero as ruler of an
assembly of gods begins to take a central place in the
values of the social structures. In short, the transi-

tion from a wholly divine natural world, run by the
gods' wills within phenomena creating a completely
"religious" response to experience on a mythic level,
moves to a largely political order, run by ruling divinities of epic stature, which Jacobsen places within the
transitions from the first to the second of the Early
Dynasties. Later, in Old Babylonian times, the peni-
tential psalms first show a further transition to the
divine metaphor of the parent caring for the individual.
Through these long periods of change, the process has
been completed from the divine as remotely impersonal
to intimately personal. Each transitional phase occupied approximately a millennium of development:

>1. An early phase representative of
>the fourth millennium B.C. and centering on
>worship of powers in natural and other phe-
>nomena essential to economic survival. The
>dying god, power of fertility and plenty, is
>a typical figure.

>2. A later phase, representative approx-
>imately of the third millennium which adds the
>concepts of the ruler and the hope of security
>against enemies. This phase has as typical
>figures the great ruler gods of the Nippur
>assembly.

>3. Lastly, there is a phase representa-
>tive of the second millennium B.C. in which
>the fortunes of the individual increase in
>importance until they rival those of communal
>economy and security. The typical figure is
>the personal god.[2]

In this study Jacobsen provides probably the best
paradigm of socio-psychic development in the transitions
of beliefs regarding man's place in the universe. After
the early myths of the dying god of fertility, a new
literary form, the epic narrative, is added. Importance
is shifted from the encompassing nature divinity of the
mythic view to the clever social ruler of the epic view.
An epic hero like Gilgamesh can even challenge the
authority of the gods. The numinous becomes centered
on the tremendous majesty and energy of the king, who
takes the place of the older ritual gods of nature. In
peace and war the driving will of the ruler replaces
the more remote powers within nature. Conversely, the
gods themselves are viewed more and more as forming a
political group, and the phenomenal world appears as a

polity.[3] The gods have gone through a transition from their "intransive" quality in a universe where everything seemed to happen by itself to their "transitive" existence in a planned universe where social laws and political order occur from the guidance of the gods in shaping local history.[4] The focus has shifted from the mythic level to the epic. Finally in the evolution of the Gilgamesh epic, the former hero is reduced to ordinary human size when Gilgamesh ironically loses the plant that could insure immortality because of his own carelessness. Gilgamesh now sees himself as a comic mortal, without any illusion about his superhuman abilities. The human being is left with his limited world of familiar place and time, without the earlier faiths in his epic grandeur or his mythic spirituality. Man is neither a hero nor a god, but only a man. From losing his illusions, Gilgamesh has grown up.[5]

By the time of the first millennium B.C., it seems that the attitude of personal piety before the divine and a deep humility in the face of man's limits have degenerated to asking the gods' favors to aid in ruthless warfare. The goddess Ishtar now is believed to help overwhelm the enemies of Esarhaddon when he succeeds in defeating his hostile brothers. From fear of Ishtar, "queen of attack and hand-to-hand fighting," the enemies' bows are broken and their battle ranks dissolved.[6] We have arrived only too evidently at the familiar level of the play for power among men, the Rhema level where man tries to have his way, disguised so that his egotistic impulses seem aided by the divine until both god and man become caricatures of what they might be.

II

The ambiguity of the human and the divine is a persistent trait in popular tradition. In contrast to Jacobsen's description of the degeneration in Mesopotamian society from heights of the divine to depths of the human, we can reverse this process to discover how the trickster figure develops from his total immaturity to full maturity. The trickster can complete the cycle that John Gardner's monster Grendel had hardly begun.

To Grendel, Beowulf appeared to be only a powerful trickster having powers the monster could not grasp. For the trickster can be both destructive and creative.

Whether we look at the trickster in metaphysical contexts or psychological conditions within folk narratives, the basic significance of his character depends on dualities, the ambiguities of opposites that comprise an unsteady unity. Our interpretation of this unstable figure also depends on the kinds of tales preserved and collected since various groups of stories may deal with radically different stages in the trickster's development. For he is anything but a constant character; rather he is extremely fluid and changeable. A view of his full career, however, must take into account his potential for evolving from an unconscious immaturity to a conscious maturity, or from a very primitive appearance to a highly civilized role.

From the metaphysical point of view, the essential duality in the trickster appears in the "two-faced" wisdom of the Brahma, one face looking outward toward the world, playing the game of good against evil, success against failure, with the full knowledge that it is a game; the other face looking inward toward the uninvolved essence, avoiding even compassion for the foolish contradictions of emotionally driven humanity. In this sense of the trickster as pure god-head, he is totally objective, outside the world, in both thought and action, and necessarily comic. But from our human point of view toward this aspect of divinity, we see him as the phoney, the confidence man. His objective essence remains unchanged, although as we see him in his progressive revelations to us he appears to grow and become humanly responsible.

From the psychological point of view, the trickster's duality at any moment in his career represents either an actual or potential transition from a primitive instinctual psychic condition entirely at the mercy of amoral impulses acting without awareness of effects on others or even on himself toward degrees of civilized rational intentions guided more and more by concerns for society with a sensitivity to the morally constructive and creatively helpful effects his typical cleverness and wit can achieve. In fact when we see the trickster as pure intelligence, he is, by his nature, creative, objective, amoral, and asocial, disciplined by none but his own laws.

For, above all, the trickster is intelligent, whether his skill is used positively or negatively, constructively or destructively. The degree of unselfish maturity is paramount in discovering what kind of trickster we find in various parts of the total popular traditions that keep the trickster's life story alive. His power and control constantly suggest the quality of a god, whether arrogant or compassionate. This divine ambivalence appears in world mythologies as the two-handed or two-faced god, or on less exalted levels as a joker, conjurer, actor, con-man, player, gambler, or trickster. The gifted mischief-maker is forever playing a joke on man.

The evasion of social responsibility in such a figure depends on the familiar axiom that the exception proves the rule, for even archaic societies are not chaotic but have their sense of propriety and order, taboo and restriction implying a religio-moral transcendence of imperfect man. The trickster figure primarily personifies the disordered life never wholly subdued by moral control but ruled by lust and hunger, pleasure and pride. Yet the trickster in his immature stages can frequently suffer pain and injury because he is a jumble of sharp cunning and childish stupidity: he fluctuates in such intermediate stages between immaturity and maturity, between selfishness and unselfishness, never quite sure of his feelings since he is trapped in his conviction that his ego is the world center. Though continually hurt, he will persist in trying to please himself at the expense of others and often delights in having an experience simply because it is not socially approved.

Implicit within his personality as well as within his relations to society are the role-playing and shapeshifting of the trickster. He plays roles by changing the masks of his persona to be successful in conning everyone to his own best advantage: to play on words for a moment, the trickster puts on masks to put people on. He is the people-watcher par excellence since he always says or does what he sees people want so that he will gain a profit for himself. What mediates his function from role to role is his clever artistry, which assumes a special morality since it is right when it succeeds and wrong when it fails. Pragmatism inevitably becomes the trickster's instinctive philosophy.

Shape-shifting, however, may be seen as more than creating deceptive appearances. In the realistic sense, the trickster appears most congenial as the hero of a picaresque mode of storytelling, each episode being a tale of outwitting his opposition for satisfactions of wealth, sex, position, or power. His escapades take

place in the world of familiar place and ordinary time
sequence. One clever trick after another might charac-
terize his career. Yet, in the perspective of psychological growth, the shape-shifting can indicate also
the evolution from quite unconscious immaturity to sen-
sitively conscious maturity. What seems a necessary,
unavoidable evil in the selfish make-up of the primordial trickster can become a willed choice for excep-
tional goodness in the unselfish, cultured clever hero.
The skillful wit can mediate between good or ill depending on the kinds of transitions available and the relative social maturity of the playful protagonist. The
trickster makes vividly clear the dramatic play within
the world of nature and men, where all is in flux,
nothing has total seriousness, everything presents the
fun of the game, a delightful activity to play for high
stakes with little regard for rules.

In cultural history, the trickster can be found
among the rich, who can afford to lose, or among the
poor, who have nothing to lose. Both have learned the
morality that you can do anything if you don't talk
about it, or you can talk about anything if you don't
do it. Only the sadly limited middle class cannot
afford the esthetic risk of playing the trickster as a
way of life. The trickster shuns the Puritan ethic of
hard work. His slothful nature exerts itself only for
advantages from its clever artifice.

The true trickster, then, lives beyond logic and
material security: his life is risk for the thrill of
winning when often he may lose. The divine and the
devilish occupy the same character; such duality is
mutually supportive since the divine creates new circumstances or pleasures through the maneuvers and mani-
pulations of the devilish. A folk tale of the Mordvins
in Central Asia illustrates this unity in diversity:
God was sitting on a rock, lonely for a brother to help
him create the world. He spat upon the waters, from
which grew a mountain. When God split the mountain, the
Devil stepped out, saying, "We will not be brothers but
companions." And together they began creating the
world.

This concept of the devil in the divinity may be
seen psychologically as the primordial unconscious of
the human being totally lost in his creature pleasures
of comfort, food, and sex; or the devil may be any
problem or opposition to his wealth and power in society, once he becomes aware of its opposition. In the

esthetic sense of dramatic interplay, the trickster
either overcomes all that prevents him from feeling
pleasant and satisfied, all desires being fulfilled,
or he defeats all obstacles to his fortune and control
by capturing each chance for getting money or sex as
often as possible. Middle-class commitments to marriage, family, friend, or child are ridiculous impedi-
ments along the trickster's creative way as long as the
trickster remains on an unselfconscious primitive level
immersed in his instinctive pursuit of success, pleasure, and survival. But, when man emerges from his
primitive intuition, he represses such egotistic urges
or compromises between ego and society. Man in his
movement toward maturity needs to be reminded of his
own tendency to fall back into vain childhood, to
recall the apprehension of losing his soul to the devil,
of subverting the holy in the obscene, for he may revert
to the darkness of his foolish youth after having
attained some light of social order.

From a tragic viewpoint this stress produces the
extremes of the ascetic who renounces the world or the
libertine who embraces the world. From the comic viewpoint the duality produces the playfully liberated
spirit of the fool or jester, laughing at himself and
at his role in the game, not a matter of life and death,
heaven and hell, but success or failure--a contest
between the stupid and the clever, where no simpleton
can play the fool. In this way, trickster tales around
the world remind us of the dangers of destructive immaturity but also of the deepest satisfactions of creative
involvements.

Through his skill, then, the trickster functions
in world narrative as the mediating agent from the
status quo, which he upsets, to a new state transformed
to his advantage, preferably without the opposition
knowing it has been tricked. Yet, ultimately the trickster tricks himself if he plays his role to the fullest
--not merely in getting his come-uppance, which may be
only a temporary justice from a stabilizing viewpoint,
but significantly in shifting his attentions from
obstacles defeating his private pleasure toward his
overcoming opposition to social welfare. As his mature
individuated self, in the Jungian sense, takes over the
role of the immature play of the ego and the id, his
pleasures become less and less ego-centered to aim now
at overcoming mankind's disorder, emptiness, loneliness,
darkness, and death. His wit can be used to defeat
such devils in society, and the highest drama of the

trickster always engages the greatest villains. The trickster at last becomes the hero of the creative myth where binary opposites of good and evil are played out for man's welfare with victory going to the clever trickster who can outwit society's devils, of greed, oppression, and abuse. The ultimate shape-shifting occurs when the infantile schemer becomes the imaginative god. The fool appears as the sage. Creativity transcends logic and common sense. The divine clown conquers.

Success comes to the man who knows how to seek within himself, among the infantile ambiguities, the insight to renew himself with each surprise of discovery within the fantastically lost situations: the wisdom of the fool who knows that to lose himself is to find himself--and all men--in the cosmic work of playful art.

III

The paradigm for the trickster in oral storytelling exists in the cycle of tales that Paul Radin collected from the Winnebago Indians in central Wisconsin and eastern Nebraska.[7] In this elaborate cycle, the pattern for the full development of the psychic energy in this figure reveals the types of stories that form the worldwide canon of episodes in the trickster's life. In his origins this character shows unbounded instinctive energies haphazardly expended. In this early stage he is the childlike person who acts from feeling and never considers the results, except to be puzzled when he sometimes injures himself. Being embedded, so to speak, in his fullest emotional capacity, he is admirable only for the vigor and vitality expended chaotically. The more his ego is at the mercy of his id, the more destructive he may be, but the happier he may feel from getting his way, for he must always come first. Within this American Indian social context, such tales help each member of the listening audience to relive stages of his psychic development and to prevent his relapsing into the dangerous phases of infantilism always threatening his emotional maturity. Something of his ambiguity exists in Chief Broom the half white, half Indian narrator of Ken Kesey's One Flew Over the Cuckoo's Nest.

To look more closely at the Winnebago cycle, then: at the beginning of these tales, the trickster-chief has sexual intercourse with a woman just before he is to go into battle, an act strictly forbidden in the

63

culture. He next insults his guests by leaving a feast
before the others have finished eating by saying there
is no point in staying when all the food is gone. When
the trickster starts on the warpath, he ridiculously
smashes his boat to discourage other warriors from following him, then sacrilegiously tramps his warbundle
of arrows into the ground to further discourage any
followers. He shows his split personality in his early
unconscious impulses when his right arm, which has killed
a buffalo, stabs his left arm, which wants to keep the
meat. Given two mysterious children who must be fed
only once a month, he deliberately feeds them often and
is completely insensitive to their deaths. Chased by
the children's father, the trickster jumps into the
ocean at the end of the world. Escaping to a shore, he
stupidly fills himself with soup made only from ocean
water since he never dips his pail deeply enough to
catch any fish. The trickster begins to be aware of
what he is doing when he realizes he has foolishly been
imitating an object that he thought was a man pointing
at him while it was only a tree stump having a protrud-
ing branch. He is beginning to see through his own
delusions about nature. But he still has far to go.

After eating several ducks that he has killed by
tricking them into dancing with their eyes closed--a
travesty on festal dancing--the trickster again shows
his disorganized, schizoid personality by instructing
his anus to keep watch over him while he is sleeping.
When foxes try to eat the trickster's duck meat, his
anus tries to discourage them with more and more explo-
sions of gas, but they will not leave until they have
finished eating all the meat. When trickster awakes,
he punishes his anus for his carelessness by burning
the mouth of the anus with a hot piece of wood from
the fire, causing him to cry out at the pain he inflicts
on his dissociated self.

After his ordeal, trickster tries to sleep but soon
wakes up and sees something like a banner flying above
him and supposes it must be the chief's banner in the
great peace feast; but he is astonished to discover that
this banner is only his blanket waving in the wind at
the end of his stiff penis, which he handles until it
gets soft. He finds his blanket at the end of his
lengthy penis after he coils it in; then he stores his
troublesome penis in a box that he carries on his back.

When he sees a chief's daughter swimming in a lake,
he weighs down his penis with a stone just the right

size so that the penis can glide underwater and lodge in her, but an old woman recognizes the trick and straddles the penis, which she chops at with an awl until she interrupts the intercourse.

In the winter, when trickster needs food badly, he transforms himself into a woman by making a vulva from an elk's liver and breasts from elk's kidneys; then he parodies the whole set of courtship and marriage customs of the Winnebago by boldly courting the chief's son, who has much food from animals he has killed in hunting, and succeeds in giving birth to three sons from the marriage. However, while teasing his sister-in-law by chasing her across a pit, some of his spare parts fall from trickster as he jumps over the pit. His identity is revealed, and trickster decides to return to his own wife. He stays with her until his son is grown but then, to avoid responsibility, he decides he must travel around the world for he is bored with his family.

His badly disorganized personality causes him much distress as he wanders aimlessly until he foolishly eats a laxative bulb growing on a bush but tries to defy the warning that it will make him defecate although he proves powerless to prevent repeated farts that blow him high into the air, followed by such a huge pile of excrement that he climbs to a tree limb to escape but slips and falls into it, making himself filthy. Blinded by filth, he bumps into one tree after another until he stumbles into some water, where he can wash himself, his blanket, and the box carrying his penis.

Trickster becomes further aware of his foolishness when he knocks himself unconscious by diving for the reflections of plums growing on a tree limb above the water. He begins to see the difference between illusion and reality, and starts to discover that there may be more to life than his bisexual deceptions and stubborn defiance of his own body.

Still, he cannot resist playing a trick on some women, whom he deceives by claiming that the tree heavily covered with red plums causes the evening sky to turn red, a mockery of the Winnebago belief that red evening sky is a symbol of death.

Another adventure occurs when trickster comes upon a dancing throng making a loud noise and he wants to join in the fun since his youthful nature is enthralled

with the shouting and drum beatings. But he can find
no one. Then he sees that the noises come from many
flies rushing in and out of an elk's skull. Although
trickster had always thought he could do anything, he
cannot enter the small neckhole with the flies. He
begins to see the limits of nature beyond his ego-
centeredness. Yet he falls for the flies' claim that
he can enter by commanding the hole to become large.
It does, and he puts his head into the skull, which
then becomes small again. He has been captured by his
conceit that he can control nature according to his
will. Although he has mingled with human beings, the
trickster is hardly beyond the limits of the monster
Grendel, as John Gardner portrayed him.

Although the trickster has remained the phoney
from a social viewpoint and a con-man from a personal
viewpoint, he has reached transitional moments of awareness and sensitivity to others, moments unsettling to
his careless impulses, spots of experience that begin
to give him some perspectives on an objective world
beyond his infantile subjectivity. But further jolts
must occur for him to be able to mediate between his
primitive and more cultivated natures. Such shocks will
make it possible for the trickster to develop a will
for creative commitment whose center is another instead
of himself.

Soon afterward in his adventures, trickster is so
annoyed by a strange song mocking at the way he packs
his penis and carries his testicles that trickster
determines to carry them correctly. The teasing voice
turns out to be that of a chipmunk representing normal
nature that has been tormenting trickster, who takes
out his penis to probe the chipmunk's hole in a log;
but when he withdraws the penis he is horrified to see
only a small piece of it left. When he kicks the log
apart in his rage, he sees his penis has been gnawed
up. But his facing the reduction of his sexual member
suddenly impels trickster to use the dismembered pieces
of it instead of letting them go to waste.

His new social orientation appears when he decides
to make objects out of the pieces for human beings to
use, such as potatoes, turnips, artichokes, beans, rice,
as well as teeth, nails, and so on. Further, this episode makes clear that the chipmunk established a better
natural adjustment since, instead of the male having
to carry his exaggerated penis on his back as trickster
had to, it is much better accommodated to its particular

function.

This transition is the central turning point in
the trickster's career; his capacities and energies
are now channeled toward improvements in nature and
culture. But because this mediating point lifts the
trickster's role to a transcendent level, beyond its
earlier limitations, the crossing of this threshold,
motivated by a socially conscious will, serves a constructive purpose in the personal and social psychology
of the audience hearing these traditional Winnebago
tales, for, as Carl Jung suggests, the primitive trickster "is a collective shadow figure."[8] The drama in
the trickster's role now takes place between the dual
poles of his psyche, whose energy depends on "the tensions of opposites." That is, the trickster undergoes
the strain of coming to terms with the biological and
psychic opposites of his persona in his shadow so that
he becomes individuated into a mature, harmoniously
integrated human being.

Degrees of improvement in trickster's life are
brought out in such episodes as his choosing to live in
a human village, where he gives up much of his bestial
nature, gets married, and makes this new place his
permanent home, never returning to the earlier village
where he had married the first time. Trickster learns
to imitate more experienced members of society like
the muskrat who turns ice into flowers, the snipe who
teaches him to fish with fibre-twine, and the wood-
pecker who knows how to catch a bear. He even tests
the previously unreliable polecat to prove that now
he always tells the truth, since the trickster is devel-
oping a conscience depending on trust between people.

After living long in the village and raising a
large family, trickster fulfills the purpose of his
creation to destroy evil spirits molesting man: in his
capacity as culture-hero he overcomes every hindrance
to Indians along the Mississippi River; he even removes
a waterfall so that people may live in its place. In
short, trickster rearranges the world for man. At the
spot where the Missouri River enters the Mississippi,
he left the land, crossed the ocean, and rose to the
heavens, where he is in charge of one of the other
worlds. From the depths of irresponsible trickery to
the heights of responsible creativity, the trickster
has discovered his divinity through using his wit and
energy to destroy evil instead of encouraging it.

IV

Some Derivations from the Folk Pattern

Aspects of the trickster-hero exist in popular narratives around the world: if the trickster is not properly a god, he is at least a super-shaman, magically controlling events for the benefit of others. His figure appears from Oceania to Africa, from Siberia to Europe. In various roles he is the African Anansi, the American Br'er Rabbit, the Greek Hermes, as well as Prometheus, and the Germanic Loki. His traits appear in the Raven of the Northeast Coastal tribes, the Coyote of the North American Plains, the Fox of Europe, and still in the Devil of Christianized cultures. In New England folklore he is found in the guises of the Yankee clowns, wits, jokers, sharpers, and swindlers, traders and pedlars, horse jockeys and practical wags, each with his degree of innocent fun or calculated villainy.

Rogues and eccentrics abound in popular literature. From the folk figures of Sam Slick to Daniel Boone, they emerge in the Dionysiac, unbounded, lawless energies in fictional heroes from the bad husband to the business shark.

In The Unembarrassed Muse: The Popular Arts in America[9] Russel Nye mentions several modern derivations. In the comic strips, the tough, vulgar Yellow Kid of Richard Outcault, the Nose-thumbing Buster Brown, and the utterly rebellious Katzenjammer Kids leave a trail of pain and destruction from their careless energy and misapplied wit. They are complete examples of the dangers in our repressed shadow nature taking over to assault all law, order, and logic. Perhaps the most perfect pugnacious, cynical con-man in the comic strips is Ignatz the Mouse, George Harriman's mouse who hits a cat with a stone and never fails in aiming a brick. Ignatz loved nobody and rejected the love of Krazy Kat, the gentle, sentimental dupe. Al Capp provided the trickster types of Senator Phogbound, the Southern demogogue, and Marryin' Sam, the phoney evangelist, while Charles Shultz dramatizes the way the world constantly cons everyone in the betrayal of Charlie Brown's faith in human nature, so that Charlie's philosophy is to dread only one day at a time. Walt Kelley added to the rogues' gallery his Albert the Alligator, a cigar-chomping blusterer with a larcenous heart and a taste for women; his public front is a fake. But

68

he is matched by the untrustworthy Mr. Mole and the pompous fraud Dr. Howland Owl. A peak of political corruption is the mean egotistical little king in "The Wizard of Id," a modern derivation of King Arthur and a super-phoney, surrounded by crafty knights, a drunken jester, shifty ladies, and an incompetent wizard.

Cleverness with betting on poker hands or on horse races probably reached a current peak in the widely popular role of Paul Newman in the film "The Sting." In the world of detective fiction, the dick had to become hardboiled to keep one step ahead of the paid-off cops, corrupt politicians, contract murderers, and expensive call girls. Society is so corrupt that the only way to survive is to play a counter-game against it. When we meet the Sam Spade of Dashiell Hammett we have come full circle in the search for the trickster who outtricks tricksters and even fools himself at times, for he was, as Hammett says, "a hard, shifty fellow, always able to take care of himself, able to get the best of anybody." Yet he is never sure if he will deny himself the broad or reject the bribe, and killing can be pleasant. Really it doesn't matter to him. His skill is to operate smoothly by knowing how to play the game in a disorderly, confused life by adjusting to it and taking care of himself instead of being defeated like McMurphy in One Flew Over the Cuckoo's Nest because he underestimated Big Nurse's trickery.

The trickster, then, represents the treacherous appearance of the ego, a necessary development toward maturity. But the forming of an ego in early childhood may mean a dangerous development if the ego remains at the mercy of the impulses for pleasure in the id. The ego-centered person lives with a psychic wall between himself and his more mature potentials. As a result the trickster narratives often reflect only the seesaw of tragicomic experiences, forever cut off from the developments of socio-psychic maturity that are expressed through the more profound visions of order in the epic and mythic versions of reality. Trapped on his Rhema level, the trickster can see nothing but the deceptions in nature or people, for to him all are out to trick him unless he can trick them first.

69

NOTES

1 Thorkild Jacobsen, The Treasures of Darkness: A History of Mesopotamian Religion (New Haven and London: Yale University Press, 1976), p. 20.

2 Jacobsen, p. 21.

3 See Jacobsen, pp. 78-81.

4 Jacobsen, p. 90.

5 Jacobsen, pp. 218-219.

6 Jacobsen, p. 238.

7 Paul Radin, The Trickster (New York: Schocken Books, 1972. First published as Memoir I of the International Journal of Linguistics, Indiana University Publications in Anthropology and Linguistics, 1948).

8 Radin, p. 209.

9 Russel Nye, The Unembarrassed Muse: The Popular Arts in America (New York: Dial Press, 1970). See Chapter Nine, "Fun in Four Colors: The Comics," pp. 216-241, and Chapter Ten, "Murderers and Detectives," pp. 244-268.

For further ramifications of subjective-objective relationships in psychological development, see Susan Deri, "Transitional Phenomena: Vicissitudes of Symbolization and Creativity," in Between Reality and Fantasy: Transitional Objects and Phenomena, ed. Simon A. Grolnick et al. (New York: Jason Aronson, 1978), pp. 43-60.

CHAPTER IV

THE AMBIGUITY OF GANDALF:

CHRIST OR BODHISATTVA?

Among the figures of fantasy, Gandalf plays shifting roles of magician, wizard, saint, and savior. Part of his ambiguity results from his evolution through the many years he lived in Tolkien's imagination. Appearing first in The Hobbit, Gandalf seems only a very wise wizard who can predict Bilbo Baggins' skill as a burglar to steal the One Ring from Smaug, the dragon who had stolen it along with other treasure from the Dwarves. In The Lord of the Rings, the more adult fantasy following the children's tale of The Hobbit, Gandalf undergoes transitions of character that place him in part among the resurrected Christ figures. Disguising himself as a meddlesome conjurer or clever trickster in his early career, Gandalf exists in a mortal body vulnerable to both weapons and magic. But after his fight with the Balrog, Gandalf can never be affected by any weapon or wizardry.

The source of his name gives some clues to his early powers. In The Mythology of Middle-earth Ruth S. Noel derives his name from the Ganndálf of the Prose Edda, where it appears among the names of the Dwarves that Tolkien used as sources for naming the Dwarves of The Hobbit. With his special power as a firemaker, shown in both The Hobbit and The Lord of the Rings, Gandalf combined the shaman's ability to build life-supporting fire with the alchemist's skill to destroy through explosives.[1]

But Tolkien's fantasy is folkloristic in a more profound way than being analogous to the Anglo-Saxon, Teutonic, and Celtic lore that Noel describes. Tolkien's universe depends in fact on such psychological transitions as the emergence from unconsciousness to consciousness or the transformation from animality to humanity, which John Bierhorst sees as fundamental to the narrative movements in the American Indian myths he studied in The Red Swan.[2] In folk myth, however, transitions may be either positive or negative, many efforts toward the positive being checked if not wholly thwarted, as Bierhorst recognizes.[3] Still, the kind of universe that Gandalf inhabits operates on the kind of compensating experience that realizes how both good

71

and bad intentions display the proverbial faith in
producing positive results, caused even to the extent
that willpower or mental states can force transformations of reality. Such internal laws operate in Tolkien's fictional world moving beyond folk fantasy, as
Randel Helms conceives Middle-earth in Tolkien's World
(Boston, 1974).

Gandalf goes well beyond such folk narrative
motifs as the "transformation of a common man to an
exalted personage" (Stith Thompson's Motif D 22) or
"god in guise of mortal" (Motif D 42). At this point,
the mythic figure of the hero as savior or the Christ
of religious tradition suggests the paradigm for Gandalf. But Gandalf's development does not fit either
Joseph Campbell's cycle of the departure and return of
the hero depicted in The Hero with a Thousand Faces
or the pattern of the folk hero that Lord Raglan
evolved in The Hero: A Study in Tradition, Myth, and
Drama. As widely dispersed figures as Oedipus, Theseus,
Jason, Dionysus, Apollo, Zeus, Joseph, Moses, and Eli-
jah in Western traditions or Watu Gunung of Java or
Nyikang of the Upper Nile reveal the pattern of a hero
being born of a virgin, with unusual circumstances at
his conception, his being spirited away to prevent his
murder since he is reputed to be the son of a god, his
being raised in a foreign place with his childhood
being completely unknown until he approaches manhood,
when he returns to his native land, becomes a leader,
prescribes laws and for a time is accepted among his
people until he is scorned and meets a mysterious death
often on a hilltop, after which his body is not buried
but he has one or more holy sepulchres. The Christ
figure fulfills most of this pattern. But such an evolution does not describe Gandalf. More significantly,
Christ's resurrection, his brief sojourn with his
followers, his ascension, and his yet unfulfilled
return in a second coming have no precise parallels
in Gandalf's experience. In popular belief, the wait-
ing for Christ's second coming resembles the expectations for the return of King Arthur or Charlemagne
whenever their people need them enough for them to
return to the world after their death.

Although Tolkien's readers know he wrote his fiction within the influence of Western Christianity, he
developed in Gandalf a fantastic figure whose pivotal
role in The Lord of the Rings remains puzzling unless
clarified by Eastern religious perspectives, especially
Buddhism. Whether or not Tolkien was fully aware of

Oriental implications in his imaginative writings, I will show how crucial events in Gandalf's career can best be interpreted from a Buddhist viewpoint.

The two crises of Gandalf's participation in the affairs of Middle-earth occur when he fights the Balrog and when he returns to continue his assistance after his apparent death.

In the first place, we find our most significant clue to Gandalf's true character, which includes a karma that will save himself as well as others, when we consider his remarks to the company of questers during his fight with the Balrog. Fully realizing the fearful threat of this hideous monster, but feeling unsure of his power to defeat him, Gandalf steels himself to face it by crying out that the Balrog cannot pass since it is a creature of darkness that will be subdued by Gandalf's secret flame. Yet, when the monster falls from the edge of the stone bridge, broken with a stroke of Gandalf's staff, it takes Gandalf to his death by a slash of its whip dragging him into the abyss. As he falls to destruction, Gandalf thinks of others more than of himself, crying out, "Fly, you fools!" To all appearances, this is the end of Gandalf. As the tale progresses, however, and Gandalf reappears, the reader may question the manner of his death. Buddhism, as well as Hinduism, may provide a clue here. For the condition of rebirth for Gandalf may depend on the last weighty words he speaks in the moment before death. The condition of his reincarnation depends on his final thought and determines the course of his rebirth.

In the second place, then, Gandalf returns as a Bodhisattva, repeating an experience that the Buddha himself taught his followers, whom he told of his past lives before he reached full enlightenment. The condition of the Bodhisattva means that he has chosen to return to the world, renouncing the state of Enlightenment in Nirvana, because he has compassion for all those who suffer in a state of existence filled with misery and suffering. The Buddha illustrated this sacrifice of the Bodhisattva in a story describing his own previous state as a monkey. Seeing a starving mother alligator unable to feed her young, the monkey provided food by jumping into the alligator's jaws. This allegory of the Buddha provides a sympathetic understanding of Tolkien's intentions for Gandalf's development. When he faces the Balrog, Gandalf at first appears almost too exhausted and weary to try to

overcome it. Without being fully aware that his self-
sacrifice will precipitate a move to a higher state,
Gandalf is stirred with compassion to save the lives of
the Fellowship. In the end, his sacrifice, like that
of the monkey in the alligator's jaws, provides the
rescue of his companions and the ultimate salvation of
himself.

Once having committed himself to this compassionate
concern, it becomes the force that causes his return.
If Gandalf had been fully non-attached to the suffering
in the world, he evidently could have passed to a state
of blissful release from all commitment to others. Gandalf shows the dilemma of the Bodhisattva between the
two methods of reducing separation between the self and
others. One is the "unlimited," following social feelings like friendliness and compassion; the other is the
way of the "Dharmas," acquiring the habit of weaning
oneself away from the "I" or "self" to regard any feeling or idea as an interplay of impersonal forces.[4] In
other words, one way is a boundless expansion of the
self; the other way is a boundless contraction of the
self. The Bodhisattva tries to live with these two
contradictory ways: the wisdom of seeing no people
and the compassion of trying to save all people.

At his moment of death, Gandalf chose the way of
compassion. By making this choice he renounced the
wisdom of impersonal non-attachment to the agonies of
life and relinquished a salvation that he apparently
deserved.

In Tolkien's manner of presenting Gandalf, he seems
not to have intended Gandalf to realize fully his high
level of spiritual attainment until after his rebirth.
Although Gandalf is an ageless figure with a youthful
vitality suggesting numerous rebirths, he does not
appear to have the full self-assurance of a Bodhisattva
when he faces the Balrog. At the point of Gandalf's
death, his sacrifice seems to have provided a momentary
postponing of the end of the Fellowship and Sauron's
capture of the Ring.

Upon his rebirth, however, Gandalf achieves a new
confidence. Although he tells of his travels between
death and rebirth, he remains silent about details, his
silence probably deriving from his awareness of how
much the fellows of the Ring are locked in suffering
through their own ignorance and desire as well as his
realization of how much he has been freed to a higher

spiritual state. Gandalf knows that telling them their
state would serve no good since they must gain such an
understanding for themselves. Now aware of his Bodhisattva level of attainment, Gandalf, delaying his own
salvation to save others, determines to remain in
Middle-earth until it is free of Sauron. While Gandalf's ultimate wisdom allows him to see no individual
persons, his compassion allows him to want to rescue
as many persons as he can. Being able to maintain these
contradictions, Gandalf becomes truly great.

Tolkien dramatizes the more confident Gandalf in
the way he meets his enemies. Wormtongue, for instance,
is soon exposed and can offer no real threat to Gandalf.
When confronting Saruman, Gandalf is confident of victory even before he knows what the Ents have accomplished. After giving Saruman a condescending lecture,
Gandalf uses both his supernatural skill and his spiritual force to break Saruman's evil, with Saruman left
fallen, probably in the hope that he will work out some
salvation in the end.

Further, when Gandalf confronts the Nazgûl at Minas
Tirith, he yields no ground to him even though the Nazgûl is clearly unaware of Gandalf's new strength. Ironically, others defeat the Nazgûl to return him to a fate
worse than the agonies of those in the Land of the Dead:
this "Lord" of the vicious host is reduced to his
ghostly state with nothing left of him except an empty
helm and hauberk, his black assistants being finally
destroyed when the One Ring is unmade.

More subtly, Gandalf perceives the true suffering
of Denethor, who fails to guard his egotistic thoughts
and exposes himself to Sauron's control. Although Gandalf tries to restore Denethor's mind after Sauron has
unbalanced him, he cannot prevent Denethor from throwing himself into the flames. Instead of rescuing him,
Gandalf probably sees the need for Denethor to have a
chance for a new life if his last "weighty thought" was
to do penance for his self-centeredness.

For the Fellowship of the Ring, the greatest spiritual adventure comes when Frodo and other companions on
the ring-quest leave for the Grey Havens. Through the
destruction of the Ring, they have overcome their ignorance and desire. Moving toward a state of Nirvana,
Frodo will no longer feel the pain of the Nazgûl blade
and Bilbo will no longer doze off in the middle of a
speech. Completely free at last, Gandalf will no longer

need his staff. Tolkien gives us a vision of the Grey Havens as an approach to Nirvana where absence of self-interest, or the achievement of final self-effacement, will allow Frodo and Bilbo to join in their ultimate wisdom, the final reality, for which Gandalf had prepared them as their Bodhisattva.

Tolkien reserves for the "appendix" of The Lord of the Rings the consolation of the earthy Sam, Frodo's mortal companion, who is seen late in life going to the Grey Havens. Legend says he joined his old friends. Somewhat too attached to the world, like most of us, Sam takes a little longer to renounce it. But the elves and the reborn Gandalf had known the true way for a long time. Perhaps, at last, Sam, the faithful friend, had himself been, without knowing it, a Bodhisattva all along.

In these ways, then, Tolkien as a profound narrator in the greatest of modern fantasies has given us a hero who remains ambiguous and contradictory if seen only from perspectives of Western myth and religion but who becomes brilliantly impressive if understood from perspectives of Oriental belief and faith. The conception of Gandalf as a Bodhisattva provides the final peak of Tolkien's spiritual fantasy.

NOTES

1 Ruth S. Noel, The Mythology of Middle-earth (Boston: Houghton Mifflin Company, 1977), pp. 108-109.

2 John Bierhorst, The Red Swan: Myths and Tales of the American Indians (New York: Farrar, Straus and Giroux, 1976), p. 22.

3 Bierhorst, pp. 23-30.

4 See Edward Conze, Buddhism: Its Essence and Development (New York: Harper and Brothers, Torchbook Edition, 1959), pp. 125-130.

CHAPTER V

THE MEETING OF THE EAST AND THE WEST

IN KAZANTZAKIS' "BOSS"

East and West, the Buddha and Zorba vibrate through the narrative that shows why, as Kazantzakis confessed, these two men had left "their traces embedded most deeply in my soul."[1] The unity of the East or the dualism of the West: man feeling as much a part of nature as branches are of trees or man believing that all nature was made for him--of such is the psychic drama Kazantzakis unfolds in Zorba the Greek.[2] Although Zorba was Kazantzakis' guru in the Hindu tradition, the Buddha was the Boss's guide in his struggle to find release from the West. Yet, as a Greek, the Boss had inherited the ways of both Apollo and Dionysus, seeming to contradict much of his Buddhist idealism. Here is the crux of the Boss's experience. Zorba's joys conflict with the Boss's torments. Zorba accepts; the Boss rejects. The dilemma can be resolved only when the Boss discovers extensions for fuller experience in the Buddhist tantric tradition that goes beyond his earlier, rarefied Buddhist mysticism. His path leads him to find not only the interplay between Apollonian and Dionysian involvements with people but also the ultimate continuity from body through mind to spirit in the organic transitions of tantric yoga. Final divinity must not be a separate entity opposing reality, the Boss finds. Neither can such divinity be "he" or "she." The Boss at last knows his personal inner peace from the salvation he must find for himself. He has to learn the freedom to feel the passionate abandon that Zorba seems always to have known. Being stirred to his depths, the Boss reaches the heights. Although the vibrant Zorba remains the valid pivot of the novel, the tortured Boss offers the fuller variety of psychological evolution.

From the Western traditions of Greece, the Boss manages to reconcile Apollo with Dionysus. From the Eastern traditions of northern India, he identifies himself with the phase of Mahayana Buddhism combining Hindu elements like pantheistic mysticism and worship of female divinities to realize his sort of Buddhahood. My study suggests how an understanding of this particular Buddhist way of life provides for the Western reader a deeper awareness of the psychological evolutions of the Boss in Kazantzakis' narrative.

Actually Kazantzakis himself shares much of the Boss's transitions toward psychic unity. Kazantzakis once wrote one of his critics that "Crete, for me, (and not, naturally, for all Cretans), is the synthesis which I always pursue, the synthesis of Greece and the Orient."[3] Implicitly Kazantzakis has the Boss pass through the stages of the Tantric Lotus Ladder, crossed by two streams of influence: the cool, lunar (Apollonian-Buddhist) energies and the fiery, solar (Dionysian-Tantric) energies. Such a development dramatized in the Boss resulted from Kazantzakis being able to assimilate the Apollonian vision of life with the Dionysian, his earlier predilection from the influence of Nietzsche on him. Through the Boss, who had adopted a Buddhist discipline for himself, Kazantzakis reveals how this refined spiritual aspect of Buddhism, so exclusively Apollonian, needs to be combined with the Tantric way to reach the kind of maturity that Kazantzakis calls "Cretan."

This particularly Cretan angle of viewing life becomes the most intimate discovery for the Boss because it was Kazantzakis' own. The difficulty of self ful-fillment appears in the perspectives that Zorba and the Boss have on each other: the Boss sees Zorba's fullness while Zorba feels the Boss's emptiness. Psychic improvement or degradation in these men depends on their feeling whether the Apollonian or the Dionysian impulse is assuming control of their masculine potentials. Each man can realize his masculinity by understanding himself in relation to the Great Mother, the ultimate measure of the feminine, experienced either as an earthly power like Rhea, whose sanctuaries in mountain caves resemble the mines that Zorba works in the hills of Crete, where the Earth Mother is felt to be benevolent, or as a transcendent power like Kali, whose sacrificial aims appear in the slaughter of the dark widow in the village, where the Destructive Female is felt as malevolent. Such oppositions suggested through the Greek Rhea and the Hindu Kali continue in the contrast between Zorba relating to the maternal vitality in the earth and the monks perverting the Blessed Mother into Our Lady of Vengeance. The confusing conflicts within the community become intense when the Boss's notion of forming an order of intellectuals is mirrored in the hypocritical monks, professing a love for Jesus, whom Zorba inter-prets as a son of Zeus and to whom the villagers pray as they slaughter the widow in a violent perversion of

Christianity.

For a long while such multiple entanglements within their lives create severe dualities of feeling for Zorba and the Boss. Both men are prevented from reaching any unity between themselves or with the villagers. When the narrative begins, the raging storm in mid-autumn impresses us as a natural reflection of the psychic upheavals pounding within the Boss's mind. The autumn time of year reflects another psychic reality from ancient Greece, for the Boss is in the middle of the transition from Apollo's reign at Delphi during the warm seasons, when the paean is sung, to Dionysus' rule at the sanctuary, when the days of singing the dithyramb are approaching. In his Apollonian abstractions where he finds no room for impure earthy urges, the Boss has been living a sober existence dedicated to pure intellectual values. He has been trying to make a paean of his life rarefied to the Apollo-Buddha psychic level that has become to him the only reality. From his concentration and discipline he has given birth to his religious concept of the Buddha in the manuscript swaddled like a child to him. But he cannot quite raise this psychic child into a god. Without any fully satisfying psychic structure, the Boss cannot decide how to finish his manuscript. Since his life is without art, he cannot put life into his art. He has succeeded in defining only a sort of immature Apollonian superiority for himself. Yet, as a Greek, he senses that life has depths as well as heights, that the intellectual cannot completely deny the physical. Tormented by this conflict, driven by his urge to find order, the Boss returns to Crete, where he hopes somehow to find himself. Something demonic has impelled him there because he tells himself, "I should fill my soul with flesh. I should fill my flesh with soul. In fact, I should reconcile at last within me the two eternal antagonists" (p. 74).

When Zorba emerges from the storm, he appears as a contemporary Dionysus. Like an anthropomorphic divinity, he can shift his roles from one trade to another. The songs he plays on his santuri create earthy music, resembling the dithyramb, as Zorba sings of warriors, butchers, lovers, and revelers. His santuri, so intimately associated with him, seems like his own offspring, swaddled like the Boss's manuscript. But, unlike the Boss's writing, this musical instrument does not torment Zorba since to him it is the "body of the beloved," projected from himself, expressing the pas-

sionate strings of his nature. When Zorba played the
santuri, his "big fingers caressed it slowly, passion-
ately, all over, as if caressing a woman. Then they
wrapped it up again, as if clothing the body of the
beloved lest it should catch cold" (p. 13). Such an
instrument, culminating for Zorba all the feminine in
life, has become a sort of Jungian anima, the comple-
tion and fulfillment of the male. When the Boss realizes Zorba's conscious joy in his music, he recognizes
in this modern Dionysus the son and lover of the female,
the psychic instrument of his salvation. "Yes, I understood," remarks the Boss. "Zorba was the man I had
sought so long in vain. A living heart, a large vora-
cious mouth, a great brute soul, not yet severed from
mother earth" (p. 13).

Once the Boss has sensed the symbolic value of the
santuri as a reflection of Zorba's balanced condition,
the songs prompt the Boss's dream fantasies. During his
sea voyage to Crete, he meditates over verses that used
to fill his mind with security and peace (p. 19).

The antitheses between "The Shepherd" and "Buddha"
in the poetic dialogue show the polarities of the Boss,
the Shepherd feeling the comforts of his hut, fire, cat-
tle, and wife, while the Buddha has no need for such
comforts. The Buddha has taught his soul to play with
him; the Shepherd is happy to play with his wife.

With these verses in mind, the Boss falls asleep
to dream of a storm ravaging the Shepherd's world, its
meadows, cows, bulls, and woman lost in the deep waters
where the Boss himself is swimming. Threatened by such
violence, the Boss feels the imperious drive to abandon
his aspiration for god-like purity. Yet he fears his
anima, the threatening realm that the passionate
dithyramb of the santuri has made fully conscious to
him. If he leaves his safe Apollonian side of his life
by trying to escape, Buddha-like, all trials and sorrows, he has only an artificial haven. He remains suspended, in Jungian terms, between his "self" and his
"shadow," revealed in his dream: the Buddha who has
filled his body with soul and the Shepherd who has
filled his soul with body.

Zorba can escape this dilemma by accepting an
imperfect world with its savagery and pain: he can
mourn with as much vitality as he laughs since he feels
that man's existence is tragicomic. But Zorba makes
the most of joy through loving, singing, and dancing.

Often only through dance can Zorba express his joy, the outpouring of the spiritual through the physical, so that his abandoned dancing like his enraptured singing is another ritualistic interpretation of himself: "in this old body of his there was a soul struggling to carry away this flesh and cast itself like a meteor into the darkness" (p. 70).

Zorba's "demon" causes his expressive impulses, whether to fight, love, work, eat, sing, or dance. Each fulfilling experience provides moments of transcendence to which he abandons himself. Zorba's life, then, has become a kind of constant music, filled with the rhythms and harmonies of his sorrows or joys, flowing in a way that appears natural to Zorba, for he is never overwhelmed by any of them. Instead he sees them as being necessary to humanity. As long as the Boss's protective sensitivity forces him to avoid any deep emotional involvement, his own Greek "demon" harasses him because he is split between his need for becoming a complete psychic whole and his egoist impulse to escape through a Buddhist denial of any passion. Instead of serenity, the Boss knows only agony:

> Obscure, pleading and imperious voices
> rose within me. I knew who was calling
> me. Whenever I was alone for a moment,
> this being cried out, in an anguish of
> horrible presentiments, transports and
> mad fears--waiting to be delivered by
> me (p. 33).

The Boss knows that madness lies in his intent to stifle living completely but also that madness lies in the Buddhist doctrine to control feeling entirely. The Buddhist ideal of removing oneself from a world of disease and death to find the peace of Nirvana may so control the emotions that one becomes a total ascetic wishing release from all worldly affections. For the Boss, his Buddhist fetters have bound him into a bond of Apollonian purity, an idealized rationality that now approaches insanity. In the presence of Zorba's robust acceptance of all, Apollonian rationality seems the greatest threat to reason. Through Zorba the Boss knows how weak his ethereal paean to Apollo appears without the earthy dithyramb to Dionysus.

But Zorba's exuberance means more than self-expression; it transforms others. This creative strength of his emotion has so completely affected Dame

81

Hortense that this aged and ugly cabaret singer finds
her life renewed: she is born again through Zorba's
amorous courtesy toward all femininity:

> It was certainly not this mumified and
> outrageously painted old woman he was
> seeing before him, but the entire
> "female species," as it was his custom
> to call women. The individual disap-
> peared, the features were obliterated,
> whether young or senile, beautiful or
> ugly--those were mere unimportant vari-
> ations. Behind each woman rises the
> austere, sacred and mysterious face of
> Aphrodite (pp. 41-42).

So the eternal male sees the eternal female.

By identifying more and more with Zorba, the Boss
has a vision of Hortense as ageless, for now he sees
"nothing was lost, no lover had died." From his more
mature understanding the Boss pictures to himself this
figure as the Eternal Feminine present to all men; she
is the Great Mother, another Rhea:

> The men came and joined her; they formed
> clusters, like amorous snakes in the
> spring, who rise hissing in a sheaf. And
> in the center, all white and naked, and
> glistening with sweat, lips parted to
> show her little pointed teeth, rigid,
> insatiable, her breasts erect, hissed a
> Dame Hortense of fourteen, twenty, thirty,
> forty, sixty summers (p. 157).

Such a return to passionate earthiness associated
with the Great Mother Rhea is enhanced by all the central personalities in this novel being joined to the
mines, the caves of earth that the Boss finances and
Zorba runs. In archetypal fashion, the Boss's imagination projects these mines as creative wombs in the fer-
tile earth, whose latest son is Zorba, another natural
phenomenon: "The earth digested and transformed its
children. The trees turned into lignite, the lignite
into coal, Zorba came . . ." (p. 109). From this reasonable, inescapable evolution in nature, the Boss can
enlarge his awareness of Zorba to a pre-mythic eternal
rhythm: to the Boss, Zorba is the son of Gaea, at one
with earth; of the earth, earthy, for all time and
place, sharing the primitive power of his mother. By

such psychic insights, the Boss has returned to the elemental awareness of classic Greek belief that Gaea was the original holder of the oracular shrine at Delphi, where Apollo made the mistake of killing the Python, a female serpent, creature of earth. In this way, the Boss is united with his own psychic counterpart, the female aspect of the male, the anima completing the animus.

The Boss had remained alien to the mine, entering only once, when a cave-in occurred, from which Zorba rescued him. The Boss has come to realize that Zorba toils in the galleries of the earth as he toils in the galleries of his mind. The dialectic of the separation between the physical and intellectual remains as long as the Boss thinks of Zorba only as the person present in his mine to dig coal, a contemporary mine-worker in Crete confined to a superficial diachronic continuity in the day's work. But, when the Boss can envision Zorba as the human being present in the earth in every place and time freed to a synchronic identity in the world's life, he is able to create a significant synthesis uniting himself with Zorba.

Beyond this resolution the Boss is further regenerated by knowing the dark, sensual widow, another Earth-Mother. The symbolic potential of woman realized in the Boss's vision of Dame Hortense becomes an intimate reality in his love affair with the widow. With her the Boss leaves his Buddhist aloofness to lose himself in passionate abandon, for within the Orientalism of this novel he moves from Buddhist meditation to Tantric worship of the living goddess as a means of salvation, or perhaps more subtly for the Boss, he has shifted from Buddhist mysticism to Buddhist tantrism. Although his lovemaking with the widow helps him achieve a psychic wholeness, he does not lose his spirituality; for he cannot become another Zorba since he retains his religious perspective in his Apollo-Buddhist aspect along with his sensuous foundation in his Dionysus-Tantrist experience.

Both loved and feared, the widow draws the Boss to her because of her magnetic strength and fertility. Although the petty villagers, dominated by patriarchal society, despise her because they distrust the matriarchal force bringing life to earth, they cannot ignore her but relieve their unresolved animus-anima conflict in their violent hatred of her. Only the aged Androulio, too old to be her lover, can respect her because of the psychic role she plays for the younger men:

> Blessed be the widow, I say! She's,
> as you might say, the mistress of the
> whole village: you put out the light
> and you imagine it's not the wife you
> take in your arms, but the widow. And,
> mark you, that's why our village brings
> into the world such fine children nowa-
> days! (p. 97)

For a time the Boss resists the widow's attraction.
He rebels against his own emotion: "I was irritated
because in my heart of hearts I also had desired that
all-powerful body which had passed by men like a wild
animal in heat, distilling musk" (p. 109). But after
completing his manuscript, his substitute for reality,
he goes to the widow, who fulfills him in love. From
Dame Hortense to the widow, the Boss has spiralled away
from his apparently shallow Apollonian restraint and
his Buddhist reserve. Yet the Boss has not relinquished
his philosophic ability to place each experience in due
perspective. After the death of Hortense and the
slaughtering of the widow, Zorba suffers great sorrow;
for in the dark widow, more than in Hortense, Zorba
has glimpsed his own source. Only the Boss can reach
an elevation of psychic distance. Through his intense
physical and intellectual experiences the Boss has
perceived the continuity from Dionysus to Apollo, from
the flesh to the spirit. The musical experiences of
the dithyramb and the paean are not antithetic but complementary, for the conscious and unconscious, the
rational and nonrational contribute to each other.

The Boss, as Kazantzakis presents him, has passed
through the stages of the Tantric "Lotus Ladder," the
seven circles or lotuses in the Kundalinī system of
yoga, the Kundalinī referring to the coiled female serpent, conceived as slumbering at the base of the spine
and needing to be aroused so that she can move to the
head whose crown is the "thousand-petalled lotus." Just
as in the Boss's life, the subtle channel along which
this serpent can pass is crossed by two streams of
influence: the stream of the cool, lunar (Apollonian)
energies of the psyche and the stream of the fiery,
solar (Dionysian) psychic energies. The problem of the
Boss's life like the task of the Tantric process is to
unite these energies and carry them along with the
uncoiling female serpent, rising from stage to stage,
from lowest lotus stage to highest, until the personal-

ity is transformed. Spiritual ascension, then, is a spiraling stream, a psychic continuity from ego to self, from conscious to unconscious, from Dionysus to Apollo.

Within the contemporary setting of Zorba the Greek, the Boss has become a kind of epitome of Apollo's shrine at Delphi, where the two gods reign, but at alternate times of the year. This eternal cycle, external in nature or internal in man, dramatized as the Tantric evolution, has eluded the grasp of Zorba. His role has been reversed with the Boss's. For now only the Boss can understand the universality of his own life. In the slaughtering of the widow, who had been his necessary female fulfillment, the Boss sees not merely a killing of a heifer in sacrifice out of fear for the ancient gods in the name of Christ. In her death the Boss experiences a restructuring of his universe: for him, time has a real meaning at last, beyond his former torment and agony, because to him "the widow had died a thousand years before, in the epoch of Aegean civilization, and the young girls of Cnossos with their curly hair had died that very morning on the shores of this pleasant sea" (p.84). Out of his demonic contradictions the Boss has won a reconciliation. In the end, ironically enough, the Boss wins the peace of Nirvana:

> . . . the widow was at rest in my memory,
> calm and serene, changed into a symbol.
> She was encased in wax in my heart, she
> could no longer spread panic inside me
> and paralyze my brain. The terrible
> events of that one day broadened, extended
> into time and space, and became one with
> great past civilizations; the civiliza-
> tions became one with the earth's des-
> tiny; the earth with the destiny of the
> universe--and thus, returning to the
> widow, I found her subject to the great
> laws of existence, reconciled with her
> murderers, immobile and serene (pp. 248-249).

In his life's rhythms, the Boss in his paean has learned the support of the dithyramb so thoroughly that when Zorba dies leaving his santuri to the Boss, the gift is a gesture the Boss no longer needs. Through the violence of his Dionysian passion, the Boss has earned his Apollonian peace. Or he has found his Buddhahood through the evolutionary transitions of the Tantra. Just as the classic Greeks learned to worship Dionysus and Apollo in the same temple,[4] the Boss has learned to

incorporate into himself the Hindu tantrism of worship-
ping his active energy as a goddess with whom he unites
as a god attaining his highest power through his union
with her. The creative transitions from Dionysus to
Apollo are reflected in the transitions from Buddhist
tantrism to Buddhist mysticism. Man and god have become
one. The East and the West have met. But perhaps
Zorba, who died on his feet, laughing at life, with no
regrets, had been there all along. Like Kazantzakis
and the Boss, we can remember his ardent humanity whenever we hear the song of the santuri.

NOTES

1 Nikos Kazantzakis, Report to Greco (New York:
Grosset and Dunlap, Bantam Book Ed., 1966), p. 430.

2 Kazantzakis, Zorba the Greek (New York: Simon
and Schuster, 1953). All quotations from the novel are
from this edition.

3 Kazantzakis, The Odyssey: A Modern Sequel (New
York: Simon and Schuster, 1958), "Introduction" by
Kimon Friar, p. xv.

4 "That the Greeks could honor the body and spirit
in the same temple was one of their most signal achieve-
ments. They adored the phallus and carried it garlanded
through the streets, and at the same time they adored
the sunlit intelligence; they saw no reason why one
should be more praised than the other, for both were
mysteries. When they went on pilgrimages to Delphi,
they might carry in one hand an arrow tipped with sil-
ver for Apollo and in the other a phallus-shaped cake
for Dionysus; and they would not have thought it
strange." Robert Payne, Ancient Greece: The Triumph
of a Culture (New York: W. W. Norton and Company,
1964), pp. 72-73.

This sort of continuity was achieved also in the
late Plato, when he shifted the accomplishment of unity
from the gods to man, so that in Timaeus "Plato may be
said to have recovered the Delphic Apollo," according
to Charles P. Bigger in "The Lesson of Apollo," The
Southern Review, 9 (Spring, 1973), p. 357.

A full description of the Kundalinī series of
lotus levels can be found in Joseph Campbell, The Mythic
Image (Princeton: Princeton University Press, 1974),

pp. 361-384. In "Seven Levels of Consciousness" Campbell describes how the <u>Kundalinī</u> process goes beyond the Western preoccupation with survival, sex, and power, reflected in Freudian, Adlerian, and Jungian psychologies. The level that seems closest to the Boss's experience is probably the sixth chakra or level, as Campbell describes it: "Within its pure white lotus is the radiant six-headed goddess Hakini, symbolizing the concentration of all five senses together with the mind. Inside the triangle is the phallus of the Lord Shiva, now pure white, supported by the sign of the syllable OM. It is here that one may behold the ultimate image of God, an image known to Christians as the beatific vision." <u>Psychology Today</u> (December, 1975), p. 78.

CHAPTER VI

MUSICAL RESOLUTIONS IN BELLOW, MALAMUD, AND UPDIKE

I

Dichotomies and conflicts at first controlled the experiences of Grendel, the monster almost reaching humanity, of Trickster, the Winnebago hero growing up, of Gandalf, the wizard becoming a Bodhisattva, and of the Boss, the European blending East and West. Each achieved some degree of unity from variety, harmony from discord. Through difficult searching, each discovered in himself the resources that produced a new vision of his destiny so that each figure resulted from the quality of imagination creating him.

Saul Bellow recently remarked in his article "A World Too Much With Us" that "the writer's true province is the unconscious . . ., the sole source of impulse and freedom." In much artistic creation, arising from the unconscious, Bellow claims, we discover what "the imagination is capable of giving" beyond the "accounts of human existence given by the modern intelligence [that] are very shallow by comparison."[1] Bellow has made explicit the structuring of the imagination in Humboldt's Gift, where his protagonist, Charlie Citrine, a successful writer, continues to search for Reality within reality by turning to music: "By means of music a man affirmed that the logically unanswerable was, in a different form, answerable. Sounds without determinate meaning became more and more pertinent, the greater the music."[2]

From the viewpoint of musical analogy, Saul Bellow and his fellow novelists Bernard Malamud and John Updike have created some of the most significant narrative structures in modern fiction. During a time when many artists have tended to regard music as the dominant art, Bellow, Malamud and Updike have successfully created esthetic effects similar to those of music whether or not they were fully conscious during their writing of the musical analogies that help the reader to become more aware of the intentions implicit in their fiction.

In this study I will suggest the effects of "theme and variations" in Bellow's The Adventures of Augie March, "arch-form sonata" in Malamud's The Assistant, and "contrapuntal texture" in Updike's The Centaur.

Each writer has created in terms of musical structure and made it his own, so that in this way it becomes a new pattern, a personal form, as Bernard Malamud maintained in his article on the "new novel": "no form dies; they are all eternally available to the artist to use in a manner original to him. He reinvents them as he uses them . . . Nothing is outdated if it creates art. The best form for an artist is that which compels him to use his greatest strength."[3]

II

Although it is not likely that Saul Bellow set out to write The Adventures of Augie March in the musical structure of theme and variations, it seems apparent that he established his theme--the tendency of human beings to enlist others in their fate--and through repetition and variation sought to reinforce his theme. In musical variations, any element may be changed as long as a sufficient number of important elements can be identified so that the theme may be recognized in each new guise. The later variations tend to depart further from the original theme, since by this time it is well established in the listener's experience: in a similar way Bellow's theme is gradually shifted from its first statement. Also, during the eighteenth century, when sonata form influenced all compositions, musicians arranged their variations in a manner following the sonata as a whole; that is, the theme and its first three or four variations formed a moderately fast "first movement" effect; the following one or two variations were in a slow tempo and different tonality, suggesting the sonata's middle slow movement; and then the remaining variations served as a faster assertive finale. Mozart, for instance, used this type of grouping in the first movement of his A major sonata for piano, K331 (in variation form) as Beethoven later structured his Thirty-two Variations in C Minor and Mendelssohn in his Variations sérieuses, Op. 54, in D minor, among others. Even today, this method of musical presentation remains the most widely used, and it appears that The Adventures of Augie March falls within this pattern.

Theme: Most musical themes are extended enough to have a definite form within themselves, and each variation follows this form. In Augie the theme falls into an ABA grouping, which every variation preserves. Bellow states his theme simply as suggested by the earthy colloquial speech of Augie's family. The theme is in a major key, as is most of the novel, and might have instructions for the interpreter: "With tenderness and good humor." Introducing Grandma Lausch as the first domineering force in Augie's life, the theme demonstrates his flexibility in carrying out orders as Grandma maneuvers him. Other members of his family, all ruled by Grandma, are presented in Chapter I, the Section A of the theme.

Section B: Chapter II comprises this section of the theme, in which there is a brief encounter with Anna Coblin, a cousin who felt it her duty to direct Augie in preparation for marrying her daughter Friedl.

Section A: Chapters III and IV return to Grandma, who lectures Augie on the bad influence of Jimmy Klein and his family, and she later shows her power by sending George off to a special school before he becomes a real problem.

Variation I: Chapters V (A), VI (B), and VII (A).

Section A: Augie matures, becoming deep-voiced and hairy, while Grandma feels robbed of her power. This variation of the theme features William Einhorn, the great manipulator who takes advantage of others.

Section B: Dingbat has his effect on Augie for a short while.

Section A: Augie returns to Einhorn, who, like Grandma, lectures to Augie against turning jailbait by choosing the wrong friend, Joe Gorham. He takes Augie to his first house of prostitution on the night Augie graduates from high school.

Variation II: Chapters VIII (AB) and IX (A).

Section A: Augie now attends college and begins to talk freely, tell jokes and have views of his own. He soon quits college, however, to move to Evanston, where he works for Mr. Renling, a sporting-goods man, and the manipulative theme is carried by Mrs. Renling who wants to groom and educate Augie.

Section B: Augie encounters Esther and Thea Fenchel. In musical terms, the mood here is suggested by Augie's feelings that the world at last has some "reasonable articulations" and "better color" when he falls for Esther. But she rejects him.

Section A: Mrs. Renling can now take over again, this time offering to adopt Augie legally and to support him through his education, but he decides to turn down her offer.

Variation III: Climax of Part I: Chapter IX (ABA).

Section A: The elaborate variation continues in a faster tempo packed with action. A short motif of crime, introduced in the theme (Augie and Jimmy Klein stole money from Christmas surprise packages), and recurring in Variation I (a robbery carried out with Joe Gorham), now reaches full impact. Gorham and the criminal influences of the Chicago neighborhood become the strong powers swaying Augie.

Section B: Augie returns home during a trip revealing further seamy sides of life when he is exposed to the starving hoboes, the homosexual in the boxcar, and the plainclothesman who takes him to the police station.

Section A: Augie ends at his boyhood home in Chicago, where his life in crime was instigated.

Variation IV: Chapter X (ABA).

This variation is the "slow movement" mentioned earlier. The tonality changes to a minor key, suggesting the destructive forces controlling Augie. "Grave" might be an appropriate indication of the mood.

Section A: Upon his return to Chicago, Augie, dirty, broke, depressed, learns that his mother has been ousted from their home and is staying in a small dark room at the Kreindls. Meanwhile Grandma Lausch has died. Simon has been in jail for starting a riot over his girl's arranged marriage.

Section B: Augie feels the influence of Padilla, though in a gentler way, since Padilla's kindness causes Augie to respond to his friendship, clinging to him, moved that he cared for him. Yet Augie becomes a book thief, avidly reading according to Padilla's philosophy: "either stuff comes easy or it doesn't come at all."

Section A: The gloom of this variation is rounded off with the news of Simon's attempted suicide followed by his plans now to marry only for money.

<u>Variation V</u>: Chapters XI and XII.

   <u>Section A</u>: Simon here becomes the manipulator.
After marrying Charlotte Magnus, he makes plans for
Augie to marry into the Magnus family.

   <u>Section B</u>: Augie becomes a close friend of Mimi
Villars, who is fiercely independent. Where previously
each person's image has been reflected in Augie--as a
melody for the piano in the right hand might be inverted
in the left--there is now no reflection, for Mimi has
no ideas for possessing and controlling Augie. Yet, as
a result of his helping her unselfishly to get out of
her predicament when she decides to have an abortion
of a child from another man, Augie is falsely accused
of being the father when a relative of the Magnuses discovers them together.

   <u>Section A</u>: Simon and the Magnus family repudiate
him.

   <u>Variation VI</u> : Chapters XIII - XIX.

      A short prelude includes Augie serving as a
union organizer and having an affair with Sophie, a
chambermaid.

   <u>Section A</u>: Now the real love of Augie's life
appears. Thea Fenchel is by far the most powerful force
on Augie among those he has known up to this point in
his development. He almost surrenders his freedom to
her. This section is expanded to include a new element,
the eagle Caligula, which throws a different light on
the relationship between Augie and Thea since Augie sees
how comically Thea fails to assert her power through
the attacks that Thea had hoped would make the eagle a
famous showpiece.

   <u>Section B</u>: A new friend, Stella, implores Augie
to help her escape from her lover, who is involved with
spreading Italian propaganda through his journal. Since
she fears what might happen to her from the criminal
underworld, Augie tries to escape with her in a car,
which breaks down and forces them to spend the night
together on blankets under the stars, where they become
lovers.

   <u>Section A</u>: When Augie returns to Thea, he begs her
to take him back, but she refuses.

Variation VII: Chapters XX - XXII.

In a freer form, and perhaps a different
tonality, this variation includes three episodes in
which Augie begins to escape over-involvement, in reaction to the preceding variation.

Section A: He considers accepting the job of
serving as companion to a former important leader in
the Communist revolution but is relieved not to have to.

Section B: Augie returns to Chicago, where he
works for Robey doing research for a book.   Here he manages to hold his own and demand sufficient money and
respect.

Section A: He considers marrying the chambermaid
Sophie but decides he doesn't care about her as much
as he had thought.

Variation VIII: Chapters XXIII - XXVI.

Section A: Augie meets Stella again and they
decide to get married.   An accompanying influence is
Mintouchian, who warns him not to expect too much of
Stella.

Section B: After the wedding, Augie leaves Boston
for overseas.   He is shipwrecked and spends a long, trying time in a lifeboat with a fellow passenger, Baste-
shaw.

Section A: Augie and Stella live in Europe because
Stella wants to.   He abandons his hopes of establishing
a home for orphans, retarded children and the old and
feeble; but he doesn't give up all hope for the future.
The composition ends on a note of optimism, with Augie
seeing himself as a kind of comic hero, a picaresque
laughing creature, going everywhere but not knowing,
like Columbus, the value of the terra incognita surrounding him.   Perhaps the seesaw of his life, brought
out by its continual ABA variations, leaves the question
open whether going everywhere may be going nowhere.

Without acceleration or fugal treatment, which
might be expected in a musical climax to the elaborate
interplay of variations, the final statement in the
narrative remains a simple theme, suggesting the earthy
quality of the opening.   But now the emergence of the
theme is more subtle and rich as it reveals the organic,

accumulated effect of all the preceding experiences in
relation to it. Augie, with us, can have the imaginative perspective of seeing that the theme of human
beings enlisting others in their fate has been transformed into a self-reliant Augie, who has removed himself from fate by laughing at it.

III

In contrast to the almost infinite variations of
man's fate in Augie March, the structuring of Frank
Alpine's life in Malamud's The Assistant depends on the
strengthening interplay of components within "sonata
form." This term, however, does not imply the form of
an entire sonata but is instead a pattern frequently
used for single movements of the sonata, often the first
movement, with its three sections: exposition, development and recapitulation. Malamud's novel appears to
suggest a modern variety of the classical sonata movement with its two or three contrasting themes in the
exposition connected by transitions, the first theme
occurring in the tonic key, the second and third in the
dominant or some other closely related key, followed by
the development extending the themes by dynamic tension,
opposing forces, harmonic modulation, inversion or dimi-
nution of themes, and the like, finally brought to the
closing recapitulation having one obligatory modifica-
tion of themes by setting the third theme (and usually
the second) in the tonic key so that the composition
will end in the same key in which it began.

In The Assistant, on the contrary, Malamud shows
a kind of modern treatment of the classic sonata by
structuring his narrative as an "arch-sonata," the one
most commonly used in the twentieth century, such as
the structure of Bartók's Music for Strings, Percussion
and Celesta and Hindemith's There and Back. In the
arch-sonata, instead of the themes being arranged in
the recapitulation according to their regular order,
ABC, the order is reversed, CBA. Using the letter D to
symbolize the development, the arch-form sonata ABCDCBA
evolves and is usually diagrammed:

                          D

               C   C

          B   B

     A   A

The themes of the exposition are the three protagonists of the novel:

Theme A: In a minor key, Morris Bober is a poor Jewish grocery-store owner, whose theme, musically, might be sad and ascending chromatically to depict Bober's uphill struggle in his drab, colorless existence. Accompanying this theme are his wife, Ida, and his daughter, Helen.

Theme B: Young, strong Frank Alpine is the second theme, in a relative major key, since, having drifted into robbing Morris's store with an accomplice, he returns to undo his crime by assisting the groceryman. Emotionally, their personal relationships now relate as a minor key and its relative major key.

Theme C: This theme of Helen, derived from her short motif in the first theme, begins to emerge in her later complex relationships to Frank.   This third theme, suggesting a possible mediation between themes one and two, completes the musical-narrative exposition.   As Morris's daughter, Helen (C) must learn to move from her father (A) to her lover Frank (B).

The development, beginning in Chapter IV, includes a variation on the father-son theme.   It is suggested when Morris and Frank begin to enjoy their talks together, with an echo when the reader recalls the loss of Morris's son Ephraim.   Variations on this theme occur with Policeman Minogue and his son, Ward; Julius and Louis Karp; Sam and Nat Pearle, all adding intensity through repetition of the father-son texture.   Also in this development section, themes from the exposition oppose one another: Frank pursues Helen with no success, then she falls for him, but she rejects him; Morris trusts Frank, then distrusts and fires him.   This narrative battlefield resembles the dynamic tensions and opposing forces in a musical development section of a sonata.   Further harmonic shifts and modulations occur in the narrative emotional depths disposed among rape, attempted suicide, and arson.   Such extensions of the development suggest the elaboration of this sonata division in Beethoven's involved treatment, breaking away from more restrained classic structure and leading to modern extravagant expressions within the sonata.

The recapitulation presents Helen after the rape-- having transferred all the ugliness of Ward's offense to Frank when he intervened--again left lonely and miserable: her tragic theme (C) emerges strongly at this point and prepares for the inverted progression of the recapitulation. In sharp contrast, Frank (Theme B) turns up to take care of the store because he wants to help Morris while the old man is in the hospital and, in this way, to reassert, psychologically and musically, the father-son stability of the structure. The final theme, which ordinarily would be "Morris," representing the melancholy opening Theme A, now becomes "Frank," whose more positive Theme B reverses positions with Morris as the recapitulation progresses by assuming Morris's role after his death and repeating with added emotional strength the drab life in detail. The extended chords at the close of the recapitulation suggest Theme A (Morris) is supported and transformed by Theme B (Frank) until the themes become one. The entire recapitulation now sounds to our imagination in an appropriately minor mode, amplified through Frank's redemption, liberating him from bondage to himself by becoming part of suffering humanity:

```
                         D

      (Helen) C              C (Helen)

      (Frank) B            B (Frank)

      (Morris) A            A (Morris)

                  IV
```

Just as structure cannot be separated from narrative or musical meaning, the interdependence of structure and style, one of the most involved problems of music, applies equally to literature. This emphasis on stylistics becomes apparent when we move from the structural complexities of Malamud's The Assistant, in which the reportorial clarity of style allows the structure to become paramount in our attention, to the convoluted style in Updike's The Centaur. Such attention to stylistic color had become typical of the Renaissance madrigal, which was "through-composed," achieving coherence and continuity by the music following verbal lines in its contrapuntal texture. The through-composed quality of the son's voice narrating the distance or the intimacy of his emotional associations with his father is supported by the thematic interweaving of Greek myth with American events of the 1940's, the combination giving The Centaur the contrapuntal texture of the madrigal.

The sixteenth-century madrigal achieved a striking resemblance to Renaissance painting with its pleasure in color, proportion, contrast, symmetry, and harmonious equilibrium. Marenzio, perhaps the greatest madrigalist,[4] born four years before Shakespeare, had an exquisite lyrical style, polished elegance, sense of color and delicate shadings of tone and emotional sensibility that can be found in Updike's mannered style of narration, as, for instance, when the son, Peter, speaks vividly of himself when he has his vision of unity in the snow:

> The shadows stream out of infinity, slow, and, each darkly sharp in its last instant, vanish as their originals kiss the white plane. It fascinates him; he feels the universe in all its plastic and endlessly variable beauty pinned, stretched, crucified like a butterfly upon a frame of unvarying geometrical truth. As the hypotenuse approaches the vertical the lateral leg diminishes less and less rapidly: always. The busy snowflake shadows seem like ants scurrying on the floor of a high castle made all of stone.[5]

Through this stylistic virtuosity, even the metaphors of the Pennsylvania farm country lend The Centaur an aura of the madrigal's pastoral quality.

At the outset of the novel its contrapuntal fabric appears with the subject (Part I of the counterpoint in the Pennsylvania town) and its counter-subject (Part II in classic Greece) being stated simultaneously: all the modern people have classic parallels. Further, delicate symmetry and balance appear in Updike's use of pairs, a mirror image suggesting the contrapuntal imitation of the madrigal. We discover, for instance, there are two car breakdowns, two nights away from home, two sexual encounters (the father George and Vera; the son Peter and Penny), two encounters with homosexuality, even two clocks and other pairings in the settings. Binary texture is established.

In Chapter II, the Part II or the second voice (myth) is omitted and Part I (contemporary reality) is treated in depth. Peter, the artist-narrator, mentions the Renaissance painters Dürer and his favorite Vermeer in their heightened everyday realism, and we begin to see the intensity of scenes and objects played off against each other.

Chapter III is myth (the second voice) with the
theme of pedagogy (the theory of evolution presented in
Chapter I by Part I) appearing here through Part II
(the mythic second voice of the two-part counterpoint).
This same scene of teacher and pupil, prevalent in Greek
tradition, has other statements in the novel: a mathe-
matical drill (Chapter I); the tutoring of a dull girl
for a geology quiz (Chapter V); and the translating of
Virgil in the Latin class by Peter with the teacher
assisting (Chapter VI). This canonic imitation throughout the novel further enhances the madrigal texture of
it.

    Chapter V, the Epitaph, serving as the mediating
focus of the novel, divides the other chapters into
equal halves of four chapters each. The madrigal's
structure is generally divided into such sections, each
being thematically developed.

    Surrounding the pivot of Chapter V, the epitaph of
the father, George, Chapters IV and VI are told by Peter
in the first person, his intimate recall ending each
time with his fearing his father's death. Extending
still further from the esthetic and psychic center,
Chapters II and VIII thematically reinforce the emphasis
on death since both chapters, again, end with the son's
fear, and both are sounded to us from Peter's boyish
sensitivity. Separating these reflecting arcs of imme-
diacy in style and emotion, Chapters III and VII are
more remotely presented; but, although they change moods
in shifts of persons and tenses, they maintain continuity in Peter's personal stylistic images: these chapters most importantly provide strong complementary
balancing of opposites since Chapter III, focusing on
Chiron, the teacher in ancient Greece, presents a fantasy of a mythic creation of the world from chaos, while
Chapter VII, focusing on George, the teacher in contemporary Pennsylvania, presents a record of a realistic
chaos in a world lacking order. Outer limits of mirrored themes in the countrapuntal texture are reached
in the all-knowing manner of the timeless humanity that
frames the composition (Chapters I and IX), juxtaposing
events and statements connected with Chiron beside those
connected with George. Although the stylistic manner is
one of ironic aloofness from the action, memories of
the distant past in Greece and the recent past in Pennsylvania fuse in a psychic unity, as when the two madrigal voices move simultaneously in this statement: "He
[Al Hummel] had been the key influence on the board when
Caldwell had got the job, in the depths of the Depres-

sion, when all the olive trees died, and Ceres roamed the land mourning her stolen daughter."[6]

At the ends of madrigals there were no codas; but it was common practice for one voice (or voices) to hold the final note while a single voice made a final statement of the principal theme. In this fashion, Updike's Epilogue is stated by Part II, the mythic depth underlying the novel. With this reversal of Parts I and II, the narrative structure is transformed for the sympathetic reader from mundane reality to spiritual belief, and the contrapuntal interplay is esthetically resolved in the strength of the single voice, the power of Zeus to elevate the neglected father among the stars.

The structure of The Centaur, then, may be visualized in terms of its divisions experienced diachronically as a V-shaped pattern, the first leg in the sequence being reflected in the second leg, as the divisions occur in spatial and psychic reflections through reading the second half of the novel. In this way we get our first impression of The Centaur as literary sequence:

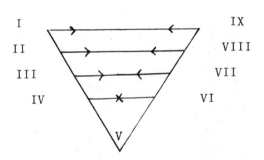

But as music the structure can be perceived as counterpoint experienced synchronically as parallel lines in which the apparent separation of contemporary America carrying the voiced theme of mortality in Part I from Ancient Greece carrying the theme of immortality in Part II is an illusion. For they are reconciled as immortality emerges and transforms the experience held in our imagination:

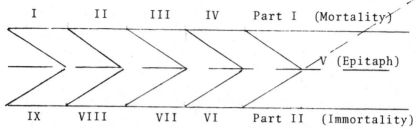

I   II   III   IV   Part I   (Mortality)

V (Epitaph)

IX   VIII   VII   VI   Part II   (Immortality)

The apparent mortality of the Epitaph is overcome
as it is silenced by the genuine immortality of the
Epilogue. Like life, the novel has its ending implied
in its beginning.

In their intuitive sensitivity Saul Bellow, Bernard
Malamud and John Updike have helped the musically aware
reader to apprehend the deeper human meanings of their
fiction.

NOTES

[1] Saul Bellow, "A World Too Much With Us," Critical
Inquiry, 2 (Autumn, 1975), p. 9.

[2] Saul Bellow, Humboldt's Gift (New York: Viking
Press, 1975), p. 332.

[3] Bernard Malamud, "Speaking of Books: The New
Novel," New York Times Book Review (March 26, 1967), p.2.

[4] Hugo Leichtentritt, Music, History and Ideas
(Cambridge: Harvard University Press, 1938), p. 91.

[5] John Updike, The Centaur (New York: Fawcett
Publications, 1964), p. 191.

[6] Updike, p. 20.

CHAPTER VII

THE COSMIC KOTO: MUSICAL FORM IN

MISHIMA'S DREAM

I

The structure of Mishima's Spring Snow follows a melodic pattern expressed through vocal music accompanied by an orchestration of such Japanese instruments as the koto (a zither of thirteen silk strings), the drum, the hichiriki (an oboe), and the shakuhachi (a flute).

Seen as a cosmic koto, the universe vibrates to the music of the spheres, confining all humanity within its immense music. Each character of Spring Snow looks out from his dark resounding chamber of personal awareness into a world of bright universal harmony. Playing his melody of search for the psychic self, each contributes his subtle variation to the theme of total perception. The organic relations among characters, dreams, and nature images create the musical structure of Mishima's novel.

The independent rationalist Honda provides the basic rhythm as an Oriental drum of persistent measured beat. Like a Shinto tune of a few notes, the elegant Satoko furnishes the recitative clarity of a finely strung koto. Sounding above the drum and strings, the protagonist, Kiyoaki, adds the arhythmic improvisational voice, searching, introspective, at times blending with the accompaniment, yet often soaring beyond it.

The fundamental impression of the search for self-awareness has the deceptively simple effect of Japanese music on the Western ear; but its many facets become evident by being played at varying intervals, modulating from the tones of dreams, emotion, and reason to the timbre of ordered time, or from twanging tradition, dissonant with present desires, to the agony of disease and death, almost annihilating but finally shading into aural hues of persisting art and beauty.

Early in the novel, the voice of the Abbess of the Gesshu Temple creates a prelude on the theme of consciousness, explaining in her parable the Buddhist doctrine of Yuishiki, which sees all existence based on subjective awareness. Her prelude sets the mood for

the simple, if tragic, romance, a fragile melody, transformed as the character of Honda, or Satoko, or Kiyoaki
gradually internalize their experiences into psychic
insights worthy of contemplation in a unified work of
art, which culminates in the Abbess's two parables serving as finale, reflecting, as in a coda, the mirror
image of the more fully conscious self.

Living as though the only valid experience comes
from successively flaring emotions, Kiyoaki dominates
this Oriental euphony with his voice, swayed by every
momentary feeling, stirred by each intimate mood. His
sung melody builds sequences from his inner life, more
real to him than any tones of the surrounding world:
even in his journal he records only his subjective
world of dreams. Vacillating from awareness of his
inner impulses to total confusion, Kiyoaki must pass
through his dark night of the soul, when even his
dreams cannot be recorded, to the mysterious, apparently
impossible goal of a mature self, like a mystic seeking
God within his own soul. The appeal of the unattainable
links many themes of the novel like a recurring motif.

Satoko, elegant daughter of an aristocratic family,
personifies the unattainable, sanctified by its distance
from reality, since Kiyoaki finds her mysteriously compelling when she becomes the fiancée of a son from the
Imperial family. Like one of his dreams, Satoko fas-
cinates Kiyoaki because she is beyond his grasp. He
finds that Satoko's melody, however, becomes increasingly complex: she expresses antithetical themes of
sanctity and sensuality, the taboo and the tempting,
the sacred and the sexual, all somehow played on the
same instrument, for the sight of Satoko makes Kiyoaki
think of a sparkling crystal or a faint note played on
a distant koto. Responding to Satoko's melodic line,
Kiyoaki hears at the upper end of the scale the sensitivity to sanctified beauty she elicits, yet at the
lower end of the scale jangles the animality he had not
known existed, a crude, sinister emotion removed from
elegance. When the vocal music of Kiyoaki combines
with the koto themes of Satoko, Kiyoaki's subjective
awareness extends to more complex intensities.

Their interplay of voice and koto is not fulfilled
as a melodic entity until joined and supported by the
drum; the steady, rational tempo played by Honda contrasts to the throbbing strings of Satoko. When Kiyoaki
shifts his attention from Satoko to Honda he moves from
her sensuous excitement into his court of reason.

Honda, though fascinated by the darkness of passion, remains as measured and cool as his weighty books of law and history. For him, reason is sunlight, emotion is blackness, and deeply ingrained in his rationalism lies an intense intuition that Kiyoaki carries the means of his own destruction. Combining intuition and intellection, Honda is able to maintain the rhythm accompanying Kiyoaki, for he can sense each direction his emotional friend is likely to take.

When Honda and Kiyoaki spend a day with two friends on the beach, Honda ponders the paradox of unity within variety:

> One could certainly think of a man not in terms of a body but as a single vital current. And this would allow one to grasp the concept of existence as dynamic and on-going, rather than as static. . . . there was no difference between a single consciousness possessing various vital currents in succession, and a single vital current animating various consciousnesses in succession.[1]

Speculating on the samsara, the ever shifting appearances of existence, Honda feels the energy in the waves as night approaches:

> The roar of the waves seemed to have grown much louder than it had been during the day. The beach and the water had each been part of their own sphere in daylight, but now they seemed to have merged under cover of darkness. The inconceivable array of stars above overwhelmed the four young men. To be surrounded by such majestic massive power was like being shut up within a vast koto.[2]

As Kiyoaki, Satoko, and Honda respond more and more to each other's tonalities and themes, they extemporize on the significance of time in their lives. Each comprehends his way of life as a different measure of time or as a special relation to time. For Kiyoaki, time becomes a force to overcome by the transcending power of love; otherwise every emotion would be bound to the physical within space. For Honda, time remains understandable on two levels, like the Yogin concept of enlightenment, since he can continue to live in his own

historical time but keep a way open into the Great Time
that is timelessness, for time appears to the philosophic Honda as only a relative concept. After they are
dead, no one will be aware of Kiyoaki's individual
voice or of Honda's own drumbeat. The essence of experience, then, can be reached at a point where time is
heard as a fluid melody, harmonious with the universal
rhythm. While Honda has an intellectually enlightend
view of time, Kiyoaki can achieve an epiphanic redemption of time only through his love for Satoko. Because
she seemed to vibrate like a musical instrument, he can
feel he has captured a special intensity of time.
Moments of deep emotion can be both timeless and
ordered, Eros penetrating Chaos.

Such an insight results from the dreamlike moment
of Kiyoaki's first kiss to Satoko, when, suspended in
timelessness and soundlessness by the colloid of snow,
they are initiated into the cosmic order, for the snow
falls about them like an ordered ritual.

Kiyoaki's tutor, Iinuma, who longs for the glory
of a heroic age, where self-sacrifice and discipline are
honored, suffers anguish trying to adjust to change.
Iinuma provides a brief discord when his longing for
old-fashioned rigidity yields to his sensual inclina-
tions as he forsakes the sweeping of the ancestral
shrine to succumb to a brutal attack on Mine in the
library he revered as a symbol of the controlled past.
The rats scurrying overhead during his tryst echo the
frantic cacophony in his brain.

Only the principal melodic line of voice, koto,
and drum seems able to reconcile dissonances between
past and present. Kiyoaki voices memories of the past
stimulated by an old sepia photograph of soldiers in
the Russo-Japanese war, recalled later in his snow-
scene with Satoko where Kiyoaki imagines the photograph
reproduced in phantom snow-figures. This fusion of
past and present within the themes of Kiyoaki and Satoko
becomes more pronounced by the support of Honda's drumbeat when he, from a distance, can appreciate the power
of love to transcend time as he recalls the lovers, the
dusty scene of the picture fusing with their bright
love. Beyond history, photographs, and all records of
measured time, Satoko and Kiyoaki rise above the dis-
sonance of past and present.

The essence of beauty sounds a prime tone in the
melodic line of Spring Snow. The dominant line of the

search for self-awareness and understanding finds major
support in the struggle for beauty and harmony; they
become, in fact, identified at times as a single motif.
Satoko and Kiyoaki, having striking physical beauty,
are beautifully matched and meant to be united. Anything opposing such harmony is evil: anything divisive
alienates beauty. In Spring Snow all elements of nature
seem to reverberate in ultimate sympathy, forming a
parallel line to the human harmony. A typical mandala
occurs with even the tiniest insect representing universal creativeness so completely interrelated that the
insect becomes momentarily the hub of the universe,
with the surrounding trees and sky, clouds and tiled
roofs created only to radiate the elegance of a beetle.
Since such beauty cannot last, Honda's logical mind
rejects it and fears such fleeting joy because it may
lead to tragedy. Seeing Kiyoaki has begun to head for
disaster, Honda asks whether life should be thrown away
as a sacrifice to a momentary beauty. That spirit of
momentary beauty, captured forever in the memory of a
glimpser from a window who sees beauty flying away like
a bird, is the essence of the art of the Japanese way
of life: a view held on a painted scroll or a timeless
intensity in a haiku. But, linked with the elegance
Kiyoaki had learned under Count Ayakura's tutelage,
there remains an indefinite feeling of melancholy. From
the time of The Tale of Genji to the present, the Japanese people have been conscious of mono no aware (the
sadness of things), the melancholy passing of everything
in this changing world. Hence Kiyoaki hears, so to
speak, poignance and poetry, sadness and sanctity in
Satoko's love, a love never fully attainable. Yet he
can live paradoxically knowing that nothing lasts forever and still finding serenity in the belief that
nothing really dies. The elegance of Kiyoaki and Satoko
will not be lost on the world: their notes in an
ascending phrase will become part of cosmic consciousness, the universal music, remaining in wait, like a
dormant lotus seed, to be played again by some other
spirits in some other time.

In all the interplay of the different musical
themes and instruments comprising the melodic lines of
Spring Snow, there is no resolution or controlling harmony in the Occidental sense. Each of the instruments
in Japanese music is heard in its own right, but without
blending or submitting to other musical lines. Just so
do the characters Honda, Satoko, and Kiyoaki move
through the novel. There is never any attempt at judg-
ing their lifestyles, for as long as they are living

intensely and artistically, each person is seen as
equally important, just as their musical counterparts
of drum, koto, and voice make equally valuable though
totally individual contributions to Japanese music.

But the musical texture of Spring Snow is deepened
by the scenes of nature as primal images to reflect
and balance the images created by the characters. Like
a set of ornamentations piped on the shakuhachi (the
flute), each evocation of a scene in nature has the
clarity and self-sustaining significance of a delicate
painting. The red maple leaves appear the color of
unpurged sins; a black dog drowned in a waterfall jux-
taposes death with the waters of life; a horse racing
through a snowstorm becomes the embodiment of the icy
breath of winter. Perhaps the most frequently played
nature scene concerns turtles, those primeval, dilatory
creatures that lie hidden beneath the waters. Like
buried images in the unconscious of Kiyoaki, the turtles
surface to consciousness only at times of insecurity.
They are a reminder of the past, of an ailing grandfather and a childhood fear. When Kiyoaki comes to
terms with this image submerged in his mind, he has
reached a new level of self-awareness, and with the
death of the turtle an era ended. Finally, the clean
clear notes of the waterfalls are a natural impression
that unites all the themes of the novel. Kiyoaki's last
dream is of the falls: he goes in memory to the source
of all life. In many religions, water symbolizes both
destruction and rebirth. For Kiyoaki, immersion in
the waters is a return to the preformal, a reunion with
the undifferentiated modes of pre-existence. His music
is not lost; it is only dormant in the waters of life.

The second interlacing instrumentation is the
recurring thematic effect of dreams. Often mysterious,
sometimes ominous, the dreams of Kiyoaki enter the
music-drama of the novel with the tone color of the low
oboe notes of the hichiriki. He dreams of golden crowns
and peacocks, symbols of royalty and nobility; the people from his waking life often enter his dreams, speaking as Kiyoaki has never heard them in life. His questing for an understanding of his spirituality comes out
in his dream of firing a gun in anger at the sky's blue
eye. When Kiyoaki's shot fells myriads of birds, they
are transformed into a tree, which could well be linked
with the Cosmic Tree. In religions from Vedic India to
ancient China as well as in Germanic mythology, a Tree
is seen as the Center of the universe, its roots plung-
ing into hell and its branches reaching up to heaven in

Nordic myth, but inverted with its roots in heaven and branches on earth, suggesting its emanation from the spiritual, as in the Upanishads. Kiyoaki's dream manifests his continual search for self-awareness and inner reality. Like Honda reflecting on the meaning of time and recorded history, Kiyoaki escapes the limits of temporality through his dreams. As Mircea Eliade remarks in his Images and Symbols: Studies in Religious Symbolism, "Dreams . . . may project the historically-conditioned human being into a spiritual world that is infinitely richer than the closed world of his own 'historical moment.'"[3] Even in waking life, the hichiriki notes of dreams can be heard, for the two most crucial scenes in the novel (the discovery of love between Kiyoaki and Satoko and the pilgrim-like quest of Kiyoaki to enter the Gesshu Temple) occur in the dreamy other world enclosed in falling snow. Like Hans Castorp in his dream-like vision in the snow (in Mann's The Magic Mountain) or like Peter Caldwell's sudden understanding of beauty in his father's life (in Updike's The Centaur), Kiyoaki has his moments of sudden meaning, his revelations of hidden truth, in the snow. Perception of beauty and truth, psychological awareness and balance are what the players on life's instruments in Spring Snow are trying to discover and express. Nowhere is their questing more poetic, more imagistic, or more revealing than in their dreams.

Dreamlike, the music of Japan may have certain recurring images that can mean different things to each listener to the music. The basic tones of Japanese music do not require the obvious contrasts and dramaticism of Western music because the hearer applies to the music his own internal vision. Out of whatever inner awareness the individual comes to achieve, he finds some meaning in the waking dream around him. He may focus on the lovely music of the thirteen-stringed koto, its ornamentations of spirituality remaining mysterious except to a few. Or he may concentrate on the singer, his vocal music a call to dreamy introspection. Whatever the dreamer hears, he will recognize that we are all on the threshold of a dream and that the music is a unified effect of a cosmic instrumentation no one can fully comprehend. Each image in the dream, each instrument in the music, each character in Spring Snow, each individual dreamer in life is equally important in his contribution to the enigmatic universal harmony.

The impression of harmonic beauty created in Spring Snow sets the tone for the remaining novels in Mishima's series of "The Sea of Fertility," the ironic, perverse title reminding us of the barren crater on the moon. The epic of reincarnation through which the spirit of Kiyoaki has passed in Honda's perception of human suffering releases us, finally, by turning all life into illusion. Questioning the reality of both life and fiction, Mishima, true to his ultimate vision, cannot rest either in his world of energy or dissipation of energy. The apparent nightmare becomes only a dream, a fiction within a fiction. Having taken us through the Japanese political intrigue in Isao, the rightwing fanatic in Runaway Horses, and the erotic affairs of the lesbian Princess Ying Chan in The Temple of Dawn, two fantastic reincarnations of Kiyoaki, Mishima ends his epic without a hero. The death of the dream has fascinated Mishima so that, in cyclic form, he returns in The Decay of the Angel, his climax of obscurity, to the unreality of young Kiyoaki when Satoko, now at eighty-three the Abbess of the Gesshu Temple, tells Honda that she had never known any Kiyoaki Matsugae. Satoko can call memory only "a phantom mirror" showing things as if they were present. When Honda, in a fog, questions the existence of Kiyoaki, Isao, Ying Chan, and even of himself, Satoko gives him her final truth: each reality appears to each heart in its own way. Honda, left alone in the Temple garden, thinks he has come to a place with no memories.

Yet the sun still flows over the quiet garden. Nature seems to continue although all of its vast activity ends in illusion. Mishima has become for the contemporary world of East and West a kind of Icarus not belonging to earth or sky, grasping neither the known nor the unknown in man's inner or outer existence, a complete void gaping between nature and humanity, since all is but a "single, blue speck of an idea."[4] Life has proved that the reality is the death of the dream.

But mankind lives by its dreams, in idea and art. For the left hand is the dreamer if the right hand is the reasoner. When he was forty-five, Mishima killed himself in a gesture of wasteful heroism, an act having sufficient reason for him, in his despair over the failure of the samurai ideal for the Japanese. Yet in his tetralogy he raises basic questions about purposes of life that may not end in the annihilation of the dream. The Buddhist doctrine of reincarnation leaves the rationalist searcher Honda in a fog of confusion as though his reason provides the only means of finding truth. As we have seen, the Buddhist faith in a Bodhisattva or the return of a savior supports such contemporary fiction as Tolkien's Lord of the Rings, and the concept of evolutionary progress lies at the base of Gardner's Grendel, where human development parallels art if it is not entirely identified with it. In the third novel of his tetralogy, The Temple of Dawn, Mishima, through the speculations of Honda, seeks to discover some moral sense in twentieth-century life. Honda becomes a guide to contemporary values through the mysteries of his experiences, which have led from the death of Kiyoaki (Spring Snow) to his reincarnation in Isao, a radical political conspirator (Runaway Horses). After Isao's failure to reform society, the next reincarnation of Kiyoaki turns out to be a beautiful Thai princess, Ying Chan. For Honda's search of spiritual meaning, however, his significant encounters in The Temple of Dawn come when he at least speculates on Buddhist and Hindu perspectives during his visits to Asia.

Being a man of little faith in anything, Honda is strongly drawn to the erotic stimulation of Princess Ying Chan, who turns him into a peeping Tom until his salacious curiosity is finally satisfied in seeing her in a lesbian embrace. The titillation of this scene epitomizes the cheapening decay of modern Japan, where Honda has fallen prey to the vulgar materialization of affluent Japan after the Second World War, his riches ending in the burning of his mansion at the foot of Mt. Fuji, its ashes falling in his expensive swimming pool like a parody of the Hindus casting ashes in the Ganges at Benares, where Honda had observed their rites.

In fact Honda has been not only a peeping Tom on the love affairs of Ying Chan but a kind of spiritual voyeur into religious traditions. The Temple of Dawn is a satire on such spiritual superficiality as well as on the degeneration from easy wealth in Japan. The imaginative sensitivity of Kiyoaki in Spring Snow is lost in the hollow pedantry of Honda in The Temple of Dawn. Honda gathers information about religious traditions but he can never feel their quality. He resembles a tourist gathering tawdry souvenirs of Siva or Buddha without any understanding of their significance. In this failure of insight, Honda has lost his Oriental heritage to become like the Occidental visitor seeing only the surfaces of the East. He participates in the degredation of modern life. Such a collapse of values is reflected in the often dry academic tone of Mishima's style in The Temple of Dawn, lacking the poetic images of Spring Snow and missing altogether the esthetic sense of a musical harmony in its structure. The Japanese art and ethos of Spring Snow have departed, leaving the sterility of The Temple of Dawn. Honda's search for mystical enlightenment degenerates into his obsessive spying on a lesbian. There is no dawn in any temple for Honda.

The heritage of ideals collapses in Mishima's bottomless "sea of fertility," summing up the modern mood of skepticism for the later twentieth century even more thoroughly than either Marcel Proust's Remembrance of Things Past or James Joyce's Ulysses had done for earlier generations. Nihilism can be carried no farther than Mishima's total disillusion. Remembering Saul Bellow's questioning of the future in the creative unconsious, we might say that Yukio Mishima has supplied the answer with a loud negation. Beyond possible monsters and nightmares is the vast nothing.

Yet the dream of mankind, in his religion and art, has been to return to some unity or harmony. Whenever the modern person retains some faith in himself, he depends on his own creative imagination to discover patterns of meaning that restore faith in humanity. Implicitly the contemporary believer in the health of the unconscious mind has a long line of speculation behind him. From the mystic who believes in any unknown God to the scientist who believes in an unknown order, we may find it hard to say which surpasses the other in nonrational zeal. In his study of man's psychic nature, The Unconscious Before Freud, Lancelot Law Whyte feared that we may enter the twenty-first century without knowing the neurophysiology of the brain and the psychology of the mind that need to be united by "a single doctrine of the coordinated structure and process of the human organ of thought."[5] In The Dragons of Eden, Carl Sagan can only suggest future evolution of the brain and hint at extraterrestrial intelligence.

From oral transmission to the dissemination of printing, we find the dilemmas and beliefs of humanity preserved for us. The socio-psychic levels described as the Rhema, Epos, Mythos and Logos of man's awareness of himself have persisted through oral and written traditions. They belong, in Sagan's terms, to the limbic, right-hemisphere of the brain, expressed by the left-hand, the "dreamer." To Sagan, they are "dream protocols, natural--the word is certainly appropriate--and

110

human responses to the complexity of the environment we inhabit."[6]   Since these visions are often mystic and occult, they escape rational proof. Perhaps this kind of harmony can be reached in the kind of cooperative processes that Sagan sees as the hope for knowledge: ". . . the aperture to a bright future lies almost certainly through the full functioning of the neocortex--reason alloyed with intuition and with limbic and R-complex components, to be sure, but reason, nonetheless: a courageous working through of the world as it really is."[7]

   The incubus of defeat need not cast a pall over our future. Whatever structures we find will be the structures in ourselves. We have evolved the mental capacities to perceive many kinds and levels of order. Whatever our limitations are, we must learn to live with them, for both art and science depend on the strengths and weaknesses of our humanity. Society has always reflected the ways in which human beings have learned to live on the psychic levels I have suggested: the world we have made for ourselves results from the interplay of the Rhema, Epos, Mythos and Logos as they have been expressed through ourselves.

NOTES

1 Yukio Mishima, Spring Snow (New York: Alfred A. Knopf, 1968), pp. 232-233.

2 Mishima, pp. 233-234.

3 Mircea Eliade, Images and Symbols: Studies in Religious Symbolism (New York: Sheed and Ward, 1961), p. 13. For the importance of creative dreaming among the Senoi in Malaysia, see Richard Noone and Dennis Holman, In Search of the Dream People (New York: William Morrow and Company, 1972).

4 Yukio Mishima, Sun and Steel (New York: Grove Press, 1970), p. 107.

5 Lancelot Law Whyte, The Unconscious Before Freud, (Garden City, New York: Doubleday & Company, Anchor Books, 1962), p. 67. In The Origin of Consciousness in the Breakdown of the Bicameral Mind, Julian Jaynes speculates on the "unconscious" directions from the right hemisphere in the brain before mankind learned consciousness. (Boston: Houghton Mifflin Company, 1976).

Max Delbruck offers further speculation on the
unity of our experience in "Mind from Matter?", The
American Scholar, 47 (1978), when he concludes "the
distinction between psychic and physical is not at all
a radical one, but a matter of degree . . . I therefore
claim that the antithesis of external and internal
reality is an illusion, and that in fact there is only
one reality" (p. 352). Our reality is what our consciousness sees. Such reality is "worlds apart from
the object" (p. 350). Opposing viewpoints of dualist
and monist arise from seeing what out language forces
us to call an object.

The kind of experience often called mystical may
be found in a union where "I become the other and become
myself," as William Johnston expresses it in The Inner
Eye of Love: Mysticism and Religion (New York: Harper
and Row, 1978, p. 47). For Johnston the Western handi-
cap of Hellenistic psychology that separates "intellect" and "will" or "senses" and "spiritual faculties"
is overcome in contemporary psychology that recognizes
states of consciousness, which can exist not only at
different times for the same person but also "concomi-
tantly in the same person in such wise that one sees
unity and diversity simultaneously" (p. 47). See also
Johnston's Silent Music (New York: Harper and Row,
1974).

The complex effects of unity and diversity in
polyphonic structure engage the attention of William
Freedman in Laurence Stern and the Origins of the Musical Novel (Athens: The University of Georgia Press,
1978). In both literature and music such polyphonic
structure makes us conscious of frequent melodic or
thematic variety that always maintains through our
accumulative memory a simultaneous harmonic relation
to the whole composition or narrative. Such psychological union suggests, once again, a Logos between these
arts.

Some more or less successful experiments with
using Oriental music in modern Occidental compositions
are described by Peter Michael Hamel in Through Music
to Self (Boulder: Shambahala, 1979). Among the most
effective, I believe, are Oliver Messiaen's modal
harmonies and John Coltrane's intuitive improvisations.
See especially Bill Cole, John Coltrane (New York:
Schirmer Books - Macmillan Publishing Company; London:
Collier Macmillan Publishers, 1976). Cole understands
John Coltrane's jazz improvisations as a spiritual

112

experience where the music as "time-occupation" creates an imaginative synthesis like a mystic marriage between content and form occurring within the artist's mind. (See Diagram C, p. 159). Such musical unity in Coltrane derives from Hindu and Chinese philosophy of music as well as from the African Yoruba and Ibo musical practice. (See p. 147 and p. 155).

In his important article on "Spacial Form in Literature: Toward a General Theory" (Critical Inquiry, 6 [Spring, 1980], 539-567), W. J. T. Mitchell places literature at a median point between music and the visual arts since it participates in music's temporal aspect and in visual art's spacial aspect. Although his emphasis differs from mine, we agree in the need to return to recognizing systematic processes of organizing consciousness (p. 566) and the ultimate Logos level of literature, which criticism should reach (p. 562).

In the same issue of Critical Inquiry (6, 1980, pp. 527-538), Robert P. Morgan shows in "Musical Time/ Musical Space" that music depends on "conventional relationships that are 'precompositional'; they exist in abstracto, in a synchronic, always present configuration" (p. 530). Out of this "abstract system of mutual relationships, existing prior to and logically independent of a particular compositional ordering" (p. 530) the composition arises. Musical tonality provides possible structure for tonal space in which musical relations and sequences occur. Musical time and tonal space depend on each other so that "the underlying structure is as important to the listener as the time-bound realities of the compositional surface" (p. 533). On the other hand, a characteristic of modern music (on my so-called "Rhema" level) is that spacial qualities occur much more on the surface of the text, where instead of transition there is juxtaposition, the music jumping between static blocks of sound, almost like masses of sound that either collide or penetrate. They can be moved about as though they are objects occupying visual space. Since the musical action takes place largely on the surface, it sounds shallow in comparison with music drawing up the deeper dimensions of substructural coordinates in transitional tonality or harmony (pp. 534-535). The more "interior" the music becomes, the more it can furnish significant moments of transition and reach its own synchronic, tonal depths. Both literature and music imply their own Logos level of unity and order.

In fact, Arnold Salop borrows literary terminol-
ogy to a large extent when he describes two basic ways
of composing music: the "narrative" and the "picturesque." (Studies in the History of Musical Style.
Detroit: Wayne State University Press, 1971). His main
effort is to show the "humanistic" effects of narrative
musical style (which means to him a sequence of structure depending on continuation, reaction, and culmination, involving intensification and the working out of
a conflicting, dramatic situation in music) compared
with picturesque musical style (which he feels as a succession of individual sections, evoking moods that are
extended to appropriate lengths and then dropped). Constructive aspects predominate in pre-Romantic music
while expressive aspects command attention in Romantic
compositions.

Nevertheless, as Calvin S. Brown reminds us, the
historical developments of music and literature have run
opposite courses: music tending to move from abstraction to representation with literature changing from
representation to abstraction. While we can discern the
shifting emphasis from Homer's external action to
Proust's internal action, or from Bach's abstract fugue
to Cage's representational sounds, music continues to
be the art mainly of form and literature mainly of
representation. (See Brown, Music and Literature.
Athens: The University of Georgia Press, 1948, pp. 268-
271).

Most recently, both composers and critics of
music have become aware of further opportunities to
experience music as vertical form instead of linear
form. They are departing from the Western preoccupation
with the tonal system, the quintessence of linearity
always moving toward tonal resolution. Such a turn to
vertical intensity, replacing horizontal progress,
recalls the chants of Tibetan monks, whose vocal music
is profoundly vertical. Other cultures mentioned in my
study, like the Balinese and Hopi, have music based on
rhythmic cycles, often repeated, since life for these
peoples does not move through dramatic intervals toward
climax. Their music is not oriented toward processes
within time building to concluding cadences. "In conception Balinese music is static, whereas ours is
dynamic and generally the expression of a crisis, a
conflict," says Colin Mc Phee ("The 'Absolute' Music of
Bali," Modern Music, 12 [1934], 164). Balinese music
is polyphonic without depending on background harmonies.
As Mc Phee observes, "The polyphonic nature of the

orchestration rises spontaneously from a musical idiom
uncontaminated by any conception of harmony. A singular
aerial sonority results, which is intensified by the
percussive nature of the gamelan" (p. 168). Balinese
music relies on intense verticality and rhythmic vitality in the total absence of harmony or modulation.

Western temporal linearity resulted from historical creations in European and American music through the
last few centuries. Such linearity is not a necessary
or exclusive base for all music since, in addition to
the Balinese and the Hopi, the Trobriand Islanders,
southern Indians, several African tribes, and the Java-
nese also have music independent of linear time gov-
erned by tonal progressions. (See Jonathan D. Kramer,
"New Temporalities in Music," Critical Inquiry, 7
[1981], 539-556.)

Such music is not teleological. (Cf. Kramer, p.
551). It cannot be experienced as phenomena or events
explained by final causes. It does not move toward an
end or ultimate resolution. It is free of the sense
of change through time because it is free from Western
concepts of cause and effect, leading to a goal. While
much music of the West shows the sense of process
through time and shares with literature the levels of
"Rhema," "Epos," and "Mythos," the "Logos" level of
music can be found most effectively in the ancient traditions of the East. Speaking of a "vertical" piece of
music, Kramer says, "A vertical piece does not exhibit
cumulative closure: it does not begin but merely
starts, does not build to a climax, does not purpose-
fully set up internal expectations, does not seek to
fulfill any expectations that might arise accidentally,
does not build up or release tension, and does not end
but simply ceases" (p. 549). Kramer's description perfectly fits Tibetan Buddhist chanting and Balinese
gamelan music, which Mc Phee observes in "Five-Tone
Gamelan Music": "Here, by means of ostinati that flow
one out of the other, and the extended circular forms
whose terminal note only marks a fresh commencement, the
Oriental conception of timeless melody with neither
beginning nor end is revealingly expressed. The beginning of the composition is no true beginning; in the
free introduction that precedes it, the soloist gives
the impression of picking the melodic outline from
invisible musicians inaudible to all but himself, to
hand it on to the musicians around him. The final tone,
moreover, is not conclusive. It can mark one more
return of the section. In the silence that follows the

end of the performance, one has the impression of the
music continuing on in still another repeat." (Musical
Quarterly, 35 [1949], 269-270.) Such music suggests the
Logos immanent in all reality. Through this music, man
perceives the timeless center of himself. "Here is
music," Mc Phee concludes, "which has successfully
achieved the absolute,--the impersonal and non-
expressive, with a beauty that depends upon form and
pattern and a vigor that springs from a rhythmic vitality both primitive and joyous." ("The 'Absolute' Music
of Bali," p. 163.)

     For further insight into connections between
literary and musical imagination, see J. Russell Reaver,
"A Comparative Study of Folktale Structure and Musical
Form," Fabula: Journal of Folktale Studies, 16 (1975),
47-56.

     6 Sagan, p. 238.

     7 Sagan, p. 238.